D1568547

ALUMINIUM ARCHITECTURE

Construction and Details

Hugues Wilquin

Birkhäuser – Publishers for Architecture
Basel · Berlin · Boston

Graphic design: Alexandra Zöller, Berlin
English translation: Gerd Söffker, Philip Thrift, Hannover

This book is also available in a German language edition.
(ISBN 3-7643-6411-4)

A CIP catalogue record for this book is available
from the Library of Congress, Washington D.C., USA

Deutsche Bibliothek Cataloging-in-Publication Data
Aluminium Architecture : construction and details / Hugues Wilquin.
[Transl. from French into Engl.: Gerd Söffker]. – Basel ; Berlin ; Boston : Birkhäuser, 2001
    Dt. Ausg. u.d.T.: Wilquin, Hugues: Bauen mit Aluminium
    ISBN 3-7643-6412-2

© 2001 Birkhäuser – Publishers for Architecture, P.O. Box 133, CH-4010 Basel, Switzerland
A member of the BertelsmannSpringer Publishing Group
Printed on acid-free paper produced from chlorine-free pulp. ∞
Printed in Germany
ISBN 3-7643-6412-2

9 8 7 6 5 4 3 2 1   http://www.birkhauser.ch

CONTENTS

AL IS SEX

Erick van Egeraat

There is a striking book, which is made of aluminium. It is titled «Sex», and was created by Madonna in 1992. It is clearly a controversial book, made by a provocative angel. Interestingly enough the book does, like almost all of Madonna's projects, make a difference. The text and the pictures portray a world of persuasive fantasies, which are unmistakably direct and powerful. And what makes the book seriously exciting and maybe even scary is that it all looks very real at the same time. This was close to ten years ago. Nowadays the images presented in that book are almost standard ingredients in today's music video clips, and the sensibility portrayed in the book is frequently used in most contemporary advertising.

Far away from Madonna's earlier sweet teenage image the book demonstrated an independence unequalled in the entertainment and media industry. Looking back at the same pictures now, they appear less shocking and slightly unprofessional, some of them even embarrassingly helpless. They come across very strong still, but they are definitely not as powerful and full of effects as the recent videoclips by Tom Jones and the Cardigans, by the Smashing Pumpkins or by Britney Spears to name a few. The same can be said of the Smirnoff commercials shown in the cinemas and on late night television. The reason for this is not just a result of improvements in photography, slicker styling or simply better production methods. Apparently we do need time to feel shameless enough to allow ourselves to appreciate a striking and challenging innovation. It takes time to vest our appreciation in new materials.

It seems an easy lesson for any kind of innovation. But there is more to overcome whenever new materials are being introduced.

The plastic shoes that were given to me by my parents in the early sixties, which resembled my father's leather sandals so strikingly, for example. They did not make me feel very good at all; not to have what I really wanted and feeling like I had to settle for second best. The shoes were okay, but the simple fact that they looked like the real thing but were not turned me off. They may have been impressive for others but they were not appealing to me. I do not share the excitement over a new production technology and definitely do not base my appreciation of the product on it. If the taste of something new just equals something already existing and is not new or refreshing it is hard to become interested in the making of it.

Driven by the need to be competitive the industry always seems to be focussed on copying, imitating or even mimicking existing and well established values. And it seems to work. It is possible to generate at least a temporary success most of the time. Not surprising, the temporariness of this kind of success is based on the downward spiral of being cheap. Looking at the plastic sandals for example, in order to satisfy all consumers they cannot be cheap enough. Something which will not be said by children who wear the newest DKNY fibre shoes, or the fabulous Nikes with their beautiful and highly decorative vulcanised tread sole. They are not just a new commercial success. These shoes are considered to represent a higher value, boosting the image of their smart and culturally aware owner. And it is products like these that finally established plastics and created the permanent and cool image of the material some forty years after its introduction.

This phenomenon does not simply exist in the media or fashion industry only. In the same way in which the plastic sandals resembled the leather ones, the concrete used in many early modernist buildings looked exactly like petrified wood. A beautiful example of this is the concrete balustrade in Michiel Brinkman's Rotterdam Spangen Housing. Painted white, the concrete used in this highly acclaimed avant-garde housing project of 1918, does everything to make us believe that the balustrade boards are made out of wood. Reassured that we are not deprived of our basic values looking at those intriguing boards we remain unaware of the real nature of the balustrade.

Fortunately nobody had this in mind when constructing the mind-blowing structure of the Hoover Dam located on the border of Nevada and Arizona. Here the concrete does not pretend to be anything else nor does it try to hide its true identity, but gives us the reassurance, the comfort and the silence which so effectfully supports the dam's image of invincibility. Characteristics like this contributed to the early recognition of the almost unsurpassable beauty of the ancient masonry structures like the pyramids of Gizeh or the Acropolis in Athens. The material in the case of the dam does not imitate, it is powerful and has a taste of strength. But did the designers of the Hoover Dam achieve what their colleagues at DKNY and Nike did? If they did then the concrete should not only demonstrate that it is the material's capacity to be strong and safe. The concrete should at least come across as something more than a slightly unattractive material. They should show the visitors that this material is not just an appropriate choice to build the dam safely but also to control its aesthetics. Exploiting the other capacities of this crude material, they demonstrate that concrete can also be soft and comforting, offering sensuality and solace. The dam's architects showed that the dam's superb structure provided time and space for contemplation and reflection, similar to the Greek and Egyptian examples.

Technological innovation and redefining its connotation can happen simultaneously. A true early example of such a work is Frank Lloyd Wright's house for Charles Ennis in Los Angeles, California. A series of highly decorated blocks that are carefully placed together forms the structure of the house and simultaneously creates that magnificent intriguing character so appreciated by Hollywood movie directors. It is exactly the capacity of these concrete blocks which makes the difference. It is the capacity to be technologically innovative as well as tasteful which makes any new material or any material that is reinvented truly exciting and attractive.

That is why the fashion industry's innovative use of materials is so challenging to consumers as well as designers. From its early image of copying and infancy, through its phase of acknowledgement as very effective and appropriate, plastics have now become the fashion statement. The material has in a period of no more than forty years reshaped our environment, our life style and most importantly our cultural awareness and appreciation. Especially today the number of these examples is almost endless.

And what about aluminium? Clearly with the help of the booming aircraft industry of the 1930s, aluminium received almost instant recognition and fully overcame its initial copying stage in its early years. But in the building industry, the use of aluminium has been confined to facade cladding systems and, whether we like it or not, more than once associated with the gloomy and uninspired buildings of the second half of the last century. Presently the number of exciting examples of innovative use has rapidly grown. Supported by the development of a more fluid architecture, in which surface and skin replace cladding, aluminium can be used at its best. Actually capable to adapt to almost any form and able to perform as structure and surface as well, the material's ultimate capacities are yet to be discovered. Whether in the construction industry it will come to be seen as the material of the future is still too soon to determine, but eventually it will be of one of those materials which make a difference.

Aluminium is also known as the «magic metal» or the «metal prodigy» because of its excellent properties both as a pure metal and also in alloy form. Aluminium and aluminium alloys are lightweight and resistant, can be machined, shaped, extruded and recycled. They can also be painted, plated and anodized as well as left untreated. They are incombustible, non-hygroscopic and non-toxic. They exhibit good electrical and thermal conductivities and, above all, are weldable.

Principal properties *(for Al 99.99 at 20°C)*

Symbol:	Al
Atomic number:	13
Relative atomic mass:	27 g/mol
Melting point:	660°C
Boiling point:	2500°C
Density:	2.70 g/cm^3
Electrical resistivity:	26.6 nΩm
Thermal conductivity:	235 W/mK
Specific heat capacity:	900 J/kgK
Lattice structure:	face-centred cubic
Coefficient of thermal expansion:	24 x 10^{-6} 1/K
Young's modulus E:	69 000 N/mm^2

The best known, perhaps the most obvious, property of aluminium is its low weight. Its specific weight is 27 kN/m^3 – just one-third of that of steel or copper. This property is easily exploited when, for whatever reason, it is necessary to reduce the self-weight of a component or group of components.

Corrosion resistance
Chemical corrosion   Although aluminium is a highly reactive metal with a very high affinity for oxygen, both aluminium itself and the majority of its alloys exhibit a high resistance to the various types of corrosion: atmospheric corrosion, aqueous corrosion and corrosion caused by oils and other chemical products. The natural «coating» of oxide makes the metal inert and so protects it from the influences of the air, temperature and humidity as well as attack by certain chemicals. Even when this layer is damaged, it forms again very quickly. In most environments the rate of corrosion decreases very rapidly with time. Only in a few cases, e.g. when subjected to sodium hydroxide solution, does the rate of corrosion remain almost constant. Although the layer of oxide is relatively thin (between 50 and 100 x 10^{-10} m), it forms a protective barrier between the metal and its surroundings as soon as the metal comes into contact with an oxidizing environment, e.g. water. The physical-chemical stability of the oxide layer determines the corrosion resistance of aluminium. This stability depends on the pH value of the environment. The protective oxide layer is stable at pH values between 4 and 8. However, as soon as the pH value rises above or drops below this range, Al^{3+} ions are formed by acidic and AlO_2 ions by alkaline (basic) decomposition. However, it is also possible to protect aluminium and aluminium alloys by means of, for example, coatings, metallic or non-metallic anodic oxidation, the use of inhibitors or cathodic corrosion protection.

Galvanic corrosion   This type of corrosion takes place when a conductive fluid bridges two chemically different materials which are joined together. Maximum damage occurs at the points of contact between the two metals because it is here that the electrical resistance is very low due to the small distance to be bridged. The points of contact between the two metals, e.g. welded, soldered and brazed joints, represent connections which can suffer from galvanic corrosion depending on the metals used. On the microscopic scale, this type of corrosion can occur between the microstructural constituents of polyphase alloys or impure metals in which foreign particles and intermetallic bonds are present. If aluminium is joined to copper or brass and at the same time subjected to moisture, then the corrosive effect on the aluminium increases. (Therefore, special care is required when the metals could come into contact with water.) Contact between aluminium and stainless steel (18 x 8, 18 x 8 x 2 and a chrome content of 13 %) causes corrosion of the aluminium even in dry environments, with corrosion being even worse in wet environments, e.g. in marine applications. Isolating the metals from each other is a simple means of avoiding galvanic corrosion. Of course, this contact can be prevented through appropriate design. However, if such contact between the two metals cannot be avoided, then it can be prevented by inserting an isolating material, e.g. neoprene.

Crevice corrosion   Narrow gaps and cracks can lead to intensive but very local corrosion; this can range from simple pitting to rusting of the entire surface. These crevices result from the geometry of the construction (e.g. riveted plates, gaps at joints, etc.), from friction between aluminium and other non-metallic objects (e.g. plastic, rubber, etc.), and from deposits of dust, dirt or the products of chemical corrosion on the surface of the metal. Inconsistent ventilation plays an important role, though not the only one, in triggering this type of corrosion. On the contrary, it is a very complex phenomenon in which acid forms in the crevices. This process is only very slow in the gaps in aluminium. The aluminium oxide which forms seals the entrance to the crevice and hence slows down the process.

Pitting   This is a very local form of corrosion which appears as dents or cavities (small elongated, conical or semi-spherical zones). Viewed through the microscope, the contours of these corroded zones are irregular. If the metal is almost completely (but not quite) covered by a corrosion-resistant protective layer, as may be the case with aluminium and aluminium alloys, then these pitted zones can occur. They arise as a result of the local cathode effect at the points where the protective layer has been mechanically damaged and cannot re-form. This type of corrosion occurs primarily when the metal is in a very damp environment (e.g. in the ground) or when drops of water or a film of condensation lie on the surface of the metal. The zones of pitting normally occur on the surfaces of metals covered in a very thin, often transparent layer consisting of inert oxides which forms either during the manufacturing process or by reaction with the environment. This can be the case with aluminium but also with titanium, stainless steel and copper. The corrosion is halted by drying the surface affected.

Intergranular corrosion   This type of corrosion involves disintegration of the grains, which leads to erosion along the boundaries of the grains. This electrochemical process depends on

Aluminium House, Toyo Ito & Associates, Tokyo, Japan

Königseder House, Helmut Richter, Baumgartenberg, Austria

Annex for Zita Kern,
ARTEC Architekten, Raasdorf, Austria

Mura-No Terrace, Makoto Sei Watanabe, Gifu, Japan

the formation of «cells» on the grain boundaries during the second phase of the precipitation. The degree to which an alloy is susceptible to intergranular corrosion depends on its microstructure, i.e. on the way in which it was produced, and on the heat treatment used. Al-Mg-Cu alloys are susceptible to intergranular corrosion under certain ageing conditions.

Exfoliation corrosion (spalling)   In this type of corrosion there is a specific and selective erosion which takes place along the numerous narrow interstitial spaces between the grains of the metal parallel to the surface of the metal. This type of corrosion is associated with a certain alignment of the microstructure. Scales and even whole sections of the surface become detached (spall off) without the involvement of external forces. Exfoliation corrosion is the most common type of corrosion with heat-treated Al-Mg-Cu and Al-Zn-Mg-Cu alloys. In those alloys susceptible to stress corrosion cracking (SCC), the effects of SCC worsen this layer-by-layer erosion. However, certain alloys not susceptible to SCC can still be affected by exfoliation corrosion. But exfoliation corrosion is generally absent from isotropic microstructures.

Filiform corrosion   These light-coloured unbranched filaments, which tend to look worse than they actually are for the structure and resistance of the metal, form on the surface of the unprotected metal or beneath the surface coatings. However, very thin aluminium alloy sheet and foil can be perforated by this type of corrosion and thin walls (as are common in aircraft construction) can be attacked, which in turn leads to a further reduction in their corrosion resistance.

Stress corrosion cracking (SCC)   Stress corrosion cracking involves the formation of cracks in an intergranular or transgranular pattern. These result from the effects of an aqueous corrosion medium – usually containing chloride – and the simultaneous application of mechanical tensile stresses. SCC can occur suddenly as a result of the breakdown of the microstructure. A material which exhibits a certain corrosion resistance in a particular environment can fail at stresses which lie below the material's ultimate strength. This is a very complex phenomenon which depends on many different factors.

Corrosion and fatigue   The simultaneous occurrence of corrosion and dynamic tensile or compressive stresses reduces the resistance to an extent far greater than the sum of the individual effects. Although it is possible to provide corrosion protection for the individual metal parts subjected to static stresses, the majority of surface coatings, including the natural layer of oxide, are damaged through fractures or cracks as a result of the effects of dynamic tensile or compressive stresses. In a corroded and fatigued state, all aluminium alloys exhibit reduced resistance in comparison to their resistance in air. For example, the resistance in a sodium chloride (NaCl) solution with 10^8 loading cycles lies between 25% and 35% of the resistance in air.

Reflectivity, thermal and electrical conductivity
Aluminium exhibits a high reflectivity to radiant energy: visible light, heat radiation and electromagnetic waves. Aluminium is a good conductor of heat; its thermal conductivity λ is approx. 235 W/mK. This figure specifies how much heat energy passes per second through 1 m² of the material with a thickness of 1 m and a temper-

MABEG Headquarters,
Nicholas Grimshaw & Partners,
Soest, Germany

ature difference of 1K between the faces. A material with a low thermal conductivity is a good thermal insulator, e.g. glass wool: $\lambda = 0.04$ W/mK, while metals exhibit very high thermal conductivities, e.g. copper: $\lambda = 380$ W/mK; steel: $\lambda = 50$ W/mK. Aluminium is a very good conductor of electricity (63% of the conductivity of copper, the most common conductor, for wires with the same dimensions). This good electrical conductivity – together with other properties of the material – has permitted aluminium to replace copper in many applications.

Fire resistance

Aluminium is incombustible. It melts when the surrounding temperature reaches its melting point of approx. 660°C. Its thermal conductivity is about four times and its specific heat capacity about twice that of steel. This means that the heat dissipates faster and hence, in order to raise a certain mass of aluminium to a specific temperature, a greater quantity of heat energy is necessary than that required for the same amount of steel.

Further properties

Aluminium is a non-ferrous metal – an important property for applications in electrical engineering and electronics. Aluminium does not cause sparks. This is especially important for many applications, among them its use in electronics and in the vicinity of explosive or flammable materials, particularly in offshore structures for the oil and gas industries. Aluminium is non-toxic and impermeable to water and air, properties which from the earliest days of its production led to its use in the foodstuffs and packagings industries. It can be shaped with pressure and/or impact loads and is easily worked using all the chief machining and shaping processes.

THE ALLOYS AND THEIR CLASSIFICATION

All the aforementioned properties are found in a wide range of alloys. The composition and categorization of all these alloys are designated by an international classification system as well as the nomenclature for wrought alloys and various national standards covering cast alloys. Aluminium and aluminium alloys are categorized as follows:
• *According to their chemical composition:*
– As aluminium with different degrees of purity, i.e. aluminium which contains only small quantities of impurities (Si, Fe, Cu, etc.) brought about by the production of the metal.
– As alloys to which particular elements have been added, the most important of these being Mg, Cu, Si, Zn and Mn.
• *According to the production method for the semi-finished products:*
– As cast alloys and wrought alloys (rolled, extruded, forged, etc.). Besides these homogeneous products, this category can also include heterogeneous products like plated products, produced by the co-rolling of different metals, and sintered products.
• *In two categories according to the type of hardening:*
– Suitable for precipitation hardening; the hardness and other mechanical properties of such alloys can be improved with heat treatment after quenching.
– Not suitable for precipitation hardening.

However, like for other metal products, another form of hardening is possible for both categories. This is work-hardening through plastic deformation in the cold state (e.g. by rolling). The following classification and standards system is one of the most frequently used. Each alloy listed is described by a four-digit number to which a letter and one further digit may be added to specify the heat treatment or the form of the alloy. For example, 6082-T6 is a moderately hard silicon-magnesium-aluminium alloy which has undergone full heat treatment.

The classification of the four digits is as follows:
1XXX   Aluminium with a degree of purity of at least 99%
2XXX   Alloys of aluminium and copper
3XXX   Alloys of aluminium and manganese
4XXX   Alloys of aluminium and silicon
5XXX   Alloys of aluminium and magnesium
6XXX   Alloys of aluminium, magnesium and silicon
7XXX   Alloys of aluminium, zinc and magnesium
8XXX   Various alloys, e.g. of aluminium and lithium

The 1XXX series is characterized by excellent corrosion resistance, high thermal and electrical conductivities, moderate mechanical properties but good machinability. These alloys are suitable for various applications in building.

The 2XXX series is highly sought after for structures which call for high strength (strength-to-density ratio). The weldability of these alloys is limited but some of them exhibit very good machinability. Alloys of *the 3XXX series* possess a strength more than 20% higher than that of the 1XXX series. However, three alloys from this series (3003, 3004, 3105) are frequently used for applications in which an alloy with moderate strength but good shaping properties and good machinability is required. These three alloys are all equally ideal for the manufacture of building components, particularly roof coverings.

The 4XXX series includes alloys which are used in welding electrodes and metal solder for connecting aluminium parts, where the weld metal has to have a lower melting point than the base metal. Alloys with a high silicon content take on a black-grey to black colouring if they are subsequently subjected to anodic oxidation. These alloys are also used in construction.

The 5XXX series exhibits very advantageous properties with regard to weldability and corrosion resistance in marine environments. These alloys are also used in architectural applications.

The alloys of *the 6XXX series* exhibit good shaping properties, good weldability, good machinability and high corrosion resistance with a moderate strength. They are also good for polishing and anodic oxidation. The alloys of this series have a range of applications in building, including welded constructions and spandrel panels.

The alloys of *the 7XXX* series are used for components subjected to heavy loads.

The letter and digit which follow the first four digits of the classification designate the various states in which the various types of products are categorized (cast or wrought alloys); ingots are excluded. The basic designations (which are further defined by the digit following the letter) are:

Commercial Centre – Le Paquebot,
Claude Vasconi, Saint-Nazaire, France

- F rough stage of fabrication with no control of the metallic structure
- O annealed stage
- H hardened by cold working (wrought alloys)
- W tempered non-stabilized stage
- T heat-treated stage

A number of other nomenclature systems deviate from the system described above. These make use of four letters and four digits, e.g. EN AW XXXX, where EN (European Norm) designates the standard, A stands for aluminium, W for wrought and the four digits are identical with those described above. The system as described above is currently being introduced as a standard throughout the EU and will replace the various national standards.

SHAPING THE MATERIAL

It can be seen from the description of their properties that aluminium and aluminium alloys are easy to shape by means of the classic metalworking methods such as rolling, extruding and casting. In addition, the surface of the material can be treated using various methods. Aluminium plate, sheet and coil material are produced by rolling. Aluminium plate produced by melting or melting down recycled aluminium is first hot-rolled and subsequently cold-rolled. This creates products with a thickness as little as 6 μm (aluminium foil). The extrusion of aluminium allows the production of sections with diverse shapes and sizes which enable a multitude of new engineering solutions. The aluminium billets are forced through a die with the aid of a hydraulic ram. Each billet supplies one or more sections, which can reach a length of up to 50 m. The sections produced are used in long lengths or cut into smaller lengths as required. These form the feedstock for cold extrusion, forging, etc. The majority of extruded parts are produced by direct extrusion. However, some are also produced through indirect extrusion. Extrusion involves applying pressure to one end of the billet at a temperature of 450°C to force the aluminium alloy to flow through the section defined by the die. All aluminium alloys are suitable for extruding. The alloys of the 6000 series (Al-Mg-Si) are the ones most frequently used.

Casting is divided into two categories:
- the casting of ingots
- the casting of finished parts

In the first method the aluminium is cast into ingots, billets, etc. which are later further processed to form finished or semi-finished products. The second method is used in foundries to produce cast parts. Two of the casting methods used are sand casting and casting in permanent moulds. This latter method can be further subdivided into pressure die-casting, low-pressure ingot moulding, spun type casting and continuous casting.

• *Surface treatments* change the appearance of the metal and provide permanent protection against the effects of corrosion. Coil coating is a continuous process in which the surface of coiled aluminium sheets is first prepared and then given a coating of (generally fluid) lacquer. To do this, the coils of aluminium sheet wound onto reels are unwound and passed through the coating bath. This process is carried out before the final shaping of the

ENT Clinic, Ernst Giselbrecht, Graz, Austria

metal. Therefore, the lacquer applied must be able to withstand the subsequent processing and shaping without being damaged. Anodizing is an electrolytic surface treatment. It increases hardness and leads to better resistance to external influences (corrosion resistance etc.), and permits the creation of polished or satin-finish metallic effects in different colours. Baking on the finish, which is even carried out on shaped semi-finished products, starts with preparation of the surface to which the lacquer, generally in powder form, is subsequently applied and firmly bonded to the metal under the application of heat. These lacquers can be divided into three groups irrespective of the type of application: PVC, polyester or polyurethane, and PVDF lacquers.

THE FURTHER PROCESSING OF ALUMINIUM

Aluminium is suitable for many metal-cutting processes, such as turning, milling, drilling, sawing, etc., for shaping processes, such as forging, drawing, embossing, folding, collar-forming, bending, hammer-forging, etc., and for jointing processes, such as clamping, screwing, riveting, welding, brazing, soldering, gluing, etc.
• *Push-fit connections* enable several parts to be connected with one or more degrees of freedom. Such connections are provided for during the design of sections and the use of other components is not necessary.
• *The clamp connection* is used primarily for fixing glass in aluminium door and window frames, for connections and protective caps. This method enables fast fitting and removal.
• *Welded joints* enable the fabrication of lightweight constructions with excellent local and global stiffness. Aluminium is one of the metals for which welding is most suitable. However, owing to its special properties, special welding techniques have to be used. As the electrical conductivity of aluminium is higher than that of steel, a higher electrical current is needed in order to produce a satisfactory welded connection. And as the metal's thermal conductivity too is much higher than that of steel, a greater quantity of heat is required for the welding process.
The aluminium undergoes a thermal change during the welding process and the material in the welding zone becomes softer and more ductile than the original metal. The expansion of aluminium upon heating and its contraction as it cools is twice that of soft steel. Molten aluminium absorbs hydrogen molecules and this can cause porosity problems in the finished weld. Prior to welding, the transparent, even layer of oxide must be removed by wire-brushing and any re-formation of the oxide layer must be prevented either by use of an appropriate flux or by the use of an arc under a protective inert gas shield. The surfaces of the pieces to be welded must be cleaned and degreased in order to remove any constituents which could contain hydrogen. Metal arc welding is hardly used these days, at best only for certain applications in which the quality of the welded seam is of secondary importance. The two welding methods most frequently used are metal inert-gas arc welding (MIG) and tungsten inert-gas metal arc welding (TIG) in which the arc and the molten metal are surrounded by a protective gas shield. These two welding techniques are carried out either manually or by automatic welding equipment. They are suitable for a whole range of alloys and different workpiece thicknesses and render possible welded

Televisa Building, TEN Arquitectos, Mexico City, Mexico

K-Museum, Makoto Sei Watanabe, Tokyo, Japan

seams of high quality for loadbearing assemblies. Pieces with thicknesses from 0.5 to 75 mm and more can be welded. The MIG method is used for welded joints subjected to normal loads; the WIG method is preferred for joints which need to fulfil higher demands.

• *Adhesive bonding.* In structural adhesive joints, the strength of the connection between two aluminium parts or between aluminium and another metal or non-metal depends on the adhesive. The three different types of adhesive which are used for aluminium are: epoxy resin, polyurethane and acrylate.

Epoxy resin adhesives are regarded as the best adhesives for structural connections. They are compatible with various metallic and other substrates. They exhibit good strength up to temperatures of 100-120°C and good resistance to the effects of chemicals. Their setting times are relatively long but can be speeded up in an oven at 80°C.

Acrylate adhesives are suitable for structural joints. Their setting times are very much shorter than those of epoxy resins. They can be used on inadequately degreased surfaces without their adhesive capacity being too severely impaired. Both epoxy resins and acrylate adhesives are very rigid and therefore sensitive to dynamic stresses, impacts and dissimilar thermal expansion between two different materials. To compensate for this lack of flexibility, some adhesives are provided with tiny elastomeric beads which are intended to stop the spread of cracks. We therefore speak of toughened epoxy resin and acrylate adhesives.

Among the large family of the polyurethanes, *polyurethane two-component adhesives* are those adhesives which exhibit good mechanical strength for structural connections, albeit lower than that of epoxy resin and acrylate adhesives. On the other hand, polyurethanes are very much more flexible and so they are used for applications in which good resistance to fatigue phenomena and vibration are required. Furthermore, polyurethanes preserve their flexibility even at very low temperatures.

Numerous research projects throughout the world are creating the foundation for the future applications of aluminium. One of the newest developments in the realm of solid-phase welding is *friction-stir welding*. In this method a tool is rotated along the joint between the two closely spaced metal workpieces. The friction between the tool and the workpieces to be joined creates heat which softens the metal at this position and produces a high-quality joint. Friction-stir welding offers many advantages: low lattice distortion, outstanding mechanical properties (in terms of fatigue, tensile and bending stresses), no liberation of gases, no porous welding zone, no metal splashes caused by the welding, no shrinkage, etc. Furthermore, this method can be used for workpieces in any position, energy consumption is comparatively low and the tool does not wear down. One tool can produce 1000 m of welded seams for alloys of the 6000 series.

The Japanese aluminium industry is carrying out research in the field of extruded components, plates with a honeycomb structure made from soldered aluminium and cast parts as components for building applications. Research into the «supermetal» have hitherto revealed that one of the best methods for improving the properties and the recyclability of the metal involves ultra-refinement of the microstructure of the metal by way of very simple chemical reactions.

ALUMINIUM IN BUILDING

Having looked at the various features and properties of aluminium as a material, it is now possible to concentrate on the use of aluminium and aluminium alloys in building. Aluminium materials are being increasingly used in the construction of buildings owing to their undisputed advantages and specific properties. However, the most significant developments have been in the field of aircraft production, notably due to the weight reduction brought about by aluminium-lithium alloys, and in the automotive industry where, with the help of finite element methods of simulation and calculation, accurate predictions of the behaviour of components made from aluminium alloys can be made, to aid the design of bodywork and chassis with integrated deformation effects. The progress recorded in these two sectors is being increasingly put to use in building.

Durability

Aluminium has a very long life even with only minimal care. Indeed, the material has an almost unlimited lifespan. The roof covering to the San Gioacchino church (Rome, 1897), components of the Empire State Building (New York, 1935), or the statue of Eros in Piccadilly Circus (London, 1893) make this point very clear. All these examples of the use of aluminium are still in a very good condition today. Aluminium does not absorb moisture, does not swell, does not rot, does not shrink and does not crack. It requires no protection against ultraviolet radiation. It does not age like organic substances. The alloys (with manganese, magnesium and silicon) most popular for architectural applications all exhibit good resistance to aggressive environmental influences and ageing phenomena. The aluminium used in construction possesses a long service life and does not need any particular care, apart from perhaps cleaning for aesthetic reasons. In aggressive environments the corrosion resistance also guarantees long-term safety even for inaccessible parts.

Average depth of corrosion in aluminium plates with a thickness of 0.91 mm

Marine climate:	after 5 years:	0.070 mm
	after 20 years:	0.085 mm
Industrial climate:	after 5 years:	0.045 mm
	after 20 years:	0.050 mm
Tropical climate:	after 5 years:	0.025 mm
	after 20 years:	0.025 mm

(source: European Aluminium Association)

One of the uses for aluminium foil and sheet is as a protective covering for other construction materials, e.g. thermal insulation. **Construction elements**   As aluminium is impermeable to water, the aluminium foil repels the water and keeps the insulation dry. Using aluminium sheet as *single-leaf external cladding* is the most obvious application for this material, providing better protection against wind and other unfavourable weather conditions for the roofs and walls of buildings. Such cladding is used exclusively as the covering to a loadbearing construction or a reinforced concrete or masonry wall. The surface may be plain or ribbed (omega, trapezoidal profiles, etc.) in order to increase the transverse stiffness.

Levi's General European Headquarters,
Samyn & Partners, Brussels, Belgium

Higher Technical Federal School, Ernst Giselbrecht,
Kaindorf, Austria

Book Technology Centre, Dominique Perrault,
Bussy-Saint-Georges, France

Twin-leaf cladding consists of an outer skin of metal fixed to a
backing plate, the inner skin. This inner leaf is attached directly
to the existing structure or an auxiliary frame which supports the
facade and transfers the ensuing forces to the loadbearing
members.

Rectangular panels – sheets generally prefabricated with plain
surfaces – are fixed either directly to the loadbearing members or
to an auxiliary frame. The fixing system is hidden.

Sandwich or compound panels are essentially complete elements
consisting of two plates – outer and inner – with a central core of
thermal insulation (polyurethane or polyethylene foam or similar).
The insulation material contributes to the stiffness of the panel and
guarantees good insulation properties. Such panels can be
manufactured in lengths exceeding 15 m and can be installed both
horizontally and vertically. The core sometimes also comprises
aluminium or plastic in a honeycomb arrangement to improve
stiffness. These panels incorporate a perimeter frame so that they
can be easily joined and guarantee sealing of the wall.

The twin-leaf facade comprises a clad inner wall which is covered
externally with a non-loadbearing glass «curtain». The two leaves
are separated by a ventilated cavity at least 150 mm wide. In actual
fact, all structural glazing elements, frame assemblies for facades,
opaque panels and all other necessary components can be made
from aluminium alloys.

The majority of aluminium construction elements are anodized or
lacquered or provided with a PVC coating. They are simple to clean
with water or neutral cleaning agents.

Strength-to-weight ratio

This favourable property of aluminium (density 27 kN/m^3) makes it possible to reduce the self-weight of a structure in certain circumstances. For the same weight, aluminium offers a greater strength (which, incidentally, can be matched to the requirements by selecting the alloy carefully – see classification) and better stiffness than other widely used materials under the same conditions. The aluminium alloys used in building possess a modulus of elasticity E of 69 000 N/mm^2 and increased ultimate strength.

In addition, the elastic-plastic behaviour of the material means that it can be classed as a safe material because sudden brittle fracture does not take place. This property is indispensable where safety is paramount, e.g. spandrel panels. Therefore, this metal is preferred for applications involving delicate but at the same time robust constructions, also those with larger dimensions, e.g. prefabricated elements for buildings, curtain walls, facade panels, glass walls and roofs, windows, doors, etc. In fact whenever stiffness is called for: installations exposed to the weather, tall buildings, large framework constructions, loadbearing assemblies. The stiffness of the metal renders possible very delicate framework arrangements which, under normal loads, do not deform.

Modern high-tech window and facade systems with good thermal insulation figures enable ecological and economic building maintenance. In their search for maximum transparency, aluminium fabricators, facade construction firms and the manufacturers of special aluminium products have developed filigree loadbearing and framework constructions. When using aluminium for the building envelope (walls, roofs, etc.), the beneficial strength-to-weight ratio is fully exploited. The low weight of the material cuts transport costs, eases handling on site and reduces the overall self-weight. Panels with a weight of 2-3 kg/m^2 can be moved manually without the need for heavy lifting equipment. Aluminium, regardless of whether or not it is now used in combination with other materials like timber, plastic, etc., is also used for sunshades, conservatories, roof coverings, handrails, aluminium foil for insulating panels, and so on.

Fire protection

Without wishing to prejudice the various national fire protection standards, we can certainly say that aluminium complies with safety requirements. It is incombustible and does not give off any toxic gases or vapours. The melting point of aluminium alloys is approximately 660°C, a temperature which is only reached when a fire is already at an advanced stage. This melting point lies very much higher than the temperature at which other building materials have already been destroyed. If an aluminium construction is exposed to a fire, then the relatively high thermal conductivity of the material means that the heat is conducted away from the zone exposed very rapidly. This aspect is extremely important when trying to reduce high temperatures around critical parts of the structure in order to maintain stability and hence prolong the period of time available for evacuating the building.

Furthermore, melting of the thin aluminium sheet of roof and wall claddings during severe fires can be incorporated in the fire concept for the building. This is because the melting process

Renault Prototype Development Centre – Le Proto,
Jean-Paul Hamonic, Guyancourt, France

destroys the cladding and so «opens» the building, thus allowing the intense heat and smoke to escape. This assists fire-fighting measures and the structure – at least for a certain time – remains intact.

Diverse design options

Aluminium offers the designer a multitude of conceptual options. The *extrusion method* permits the production of an infinite range of different solid or hollow sections which possess the necessary properties for the intended application and can be manufactured to tolerances of the order of magnitude of just a few hundredths of a millimetre. A vast range of extruded sections is possible; from sections primarily designed to meet aesthetic demands (e.g. rectangular, circular, oval and other cross-sections) to sections required to meet technical requirements (to accommodate clamped connections, slots for joining to other components, interruptions to thermal bridges, channels for condensation, frames for glazing systems, etc.). The technological progress which has been achieved in the design of extrusion plant and the extrusion process as well as improvements in productivity have set new standards with respect to the imperviousness to air and water. The fact that the extrusion process for aluminium alloys is simple to use makes it possible to utilize the metal exactly where it really is of benefit. This represents another advantage with respect to the cost of the material. The adaptability compensates for the disadvantage that the modulus of elasticity of aluminium and aluminium alloys is only one third that of steel. If you strengthen an aluminium beam by 50 %, then it is possible to achieve the strength of steel – and that for just half the self-weight. When using extruded aluminium products it is also not difficult to create sections with which the torsional strength can be improved while at the same time including openings for cables or pipes, slots for fixing intermediate floors, etc.

The relatively low cost of an aluminium extrusion tool (1500), the ever shorter set-up times in the extrusion plant and the possibility of fabricating just small amounts of aluminium (a few hundred kilograms), renders possible the production of custom sections even for comparatively small projects. Panels for diverse cladding applications (facades, roofs) may be flat, curved or profiled. Special shaping can be carried out on site with the help of a portable shaping tool. Bespoke aluminium components can also be cast. Aluminium may be sawn, drilled, folded, bent, joined, welded, etc., both in the factory and on the building site. Furthermore, aluminium can be given diverse treatments. As already mentioned, anodizing and lacquering are the finishes most frequently employed. Anodizing involves creating a natural or coloured oxide layer on the surface with the help of an electrolytic process. Initially there were only three options (natural, bronze or champagne colour), but in the meantime other colours with metallic or mineral glitter effects (pyrite) have been developed. Anodizing with a two-tone effect (the colour changes depending on the incidence of the light) has also been used on a number of buildings, notably in Japan.

Lacquering, often with the help of an electrostatic powder coating technique followed by a hardening process in a furnace, is carried out on individual parts or on continuous sheet (coil coating). The use of polyester lacquer, baked on in a furnace, is widely used for achieving a diverse range of colours and effects. The recent

Arts and Cultural Centre – La Filature, Claude Vasconi, Mulhouse, France

Mercedes-Benz Design Center, Renzo Piano Building Workshop, Sindelfingen, Germany

Convention Centre, Claude Vasconi, Reims, France

Redevelopment of Borsig Works, Claude Vasconi,
Berlin, Germany

appearance of lacquers with granular or metallic effects leads us to assume that further new developments are in the pipeline. Various manufacturers are treading new ground in the treatment of aluminium parts, e.g. the use of bonded coatings of wooden laminates.

Thermal performance

Energy losses from a building consist of transmission and ventilation heating losses. Aluminium is a good conductor of heat. Therefore, various measures have to be employed in order to prevent thermal bridges in the various applications. The good dimensional stability of the components and, above all, the aluminium sections (low thermal expansion, no flaws in the material) guarantee long-term imperviousness to water and air.

Window and door frames made from aluminium generally consist of two half-sections sandwiching a thermal insulation material chosen because of its stiffness, dimensional stability and long useful life (polyamides, resins, etc.). The inside face of the element is thermally isolated from the outside face in order to reduce energy losses to a minimum; further, raising the temperature of the inner surfaces prevents the formation of condensation. The well-sealed joints ensure the airtightness of the frames. Therefore, transmission and ventilation heating losses take place at the junctions with the components of the overall structure. It is therefore absolutely essential to ensure careful installation with permanently sealed joints as well as an overall structure or construction without thermal bridges. Aluminium sections are of course primarily used with twin-leaf or multileaf ventilated facades.

Facade claddings sometimes exhibit weak points in terms of thermal insulation at the connections between the external sheeting and the internal loadbearing construction, either due to the unavoidable mechanical fixing or excessive compression of the insulation at such points. Further, if the inner face of the multileaf wall construction is not sealed or insufficiently sealed, then the internal air – provided it is at a higher pressure – permeates the facade construction and heats up the inner face of the external sheeting. If the temperature of the external sheeting remains below the dewpoint temperature despite this heating, then condensation forms and is trapped within the construction. Therefore, dense thermal insulation well bonded to the metal cladding is absolutely vital in order to avoid internal thermal convection around and through the insulation which can considerably reduce the thermal properties of the material (up to 50%). The only answer to excessive cooling of the external cladding (i.e. the surface temperature dropping to a temperature below that of the air) and hence the possible formation of condensation on the inner face of the external sheeting (which is completely inaccessible) is so-called non-ventilated construction – airtight, single-skin roofs known as warm decks.

One design of warm deck in aluminium makes use of standing seams. These tray-type panels are mounted on anchor sections of extruded aluminium and fixed to the loadbearing construction with the help of an isolating beam bracket. Thermal convection is prevented by the well-sealed construction. To do this, the insulation is first installed with a thickness allowance and afterwards compressed to the right thickness upon laying the roofing panels.

Hong Kong Convention and Exhibition Center,
SOM and Wong & Ouyang, Hong Kong, China

Greenwich Transport Interchange, Foster & Partners,
Greenwich, Great Britain

Brussels Exhibition Centre, Samyn & Partners, Brussels, Belgium

The standing seams are folded by machine. This method of fixing
without openings to the outside guarantees optimum airtightness
and permits unhindered thermal expansion of the sheeting. The
vapour barrier must be carefully bonded so that no moisture can
permeate from the inside into the roof covering when a suction
pressure is generated outside by the wind.

The ecological advantages

The *recyclability* of aluminium is one of its most important qualities.
After demolition of a building, the aluminium products can be used
again, indeed without any loss in terms of quality or the properties
of the primary material. The use of recycled aluminium also leads to
significant energy-savings, as was mentioned earlier. (Melting down
used aluminium components requires only 5% of the energy
necessary to produce new metal.) Another plus is that the low
weight of the material leads not only to lower energy consumption
during processing, transport and handling, but also means lighter
structures and hence less material consumed in the foundations.

THE HISTORY OF THE MATERIAL

Aluminium was first isolated in the early 19th century. In the natural state aluminium is found in most types of rock, in clay, soils, etc., but always combined with oxygen or other elements. It only exists in combination with other substances, like silicates and/or oxides. These compounds are very stable and therefore it required many years of research and work before the metal itself could be separated out. Early civilizations used, in particular, clay containing aluminium (hydrated aluminium silicates) for the production of pottery, and in ancient times the Egyptians and Babylonians made use of aluminium salts for creating their pigments and medicines (as a remedy for indigestion, as toothpaste, etc.). The ancient Greeks and the Romans used alum in order to make astringent or desiccative products. Alum is a chemical compound consisting of water molecules and two types of salt, one of which is usually aluminium sulphate $Al_2(SO_4)_3$. Potash alum has the chemical formula $K_2SO_4 \cdot Al_2(SO_4)_3 \cdot 24H_2O$. Other types of alum comprise aluminium sulphates, including sodium alum, ammonia alum and silver alum.

In the Middle Ages aluminium was one of the elements which acquired an alchemy symbol. In 1761 Henri Louis Duhamel from Monceau introduced the name «alumina» for all substances based on alum. In 1808 the English chemist Sir Humphry Davy finally established the existence of the metal and called it «aluminum», a designation which later became «aluminium». He tried to decompose alumina (aluminium oxide) with the aid of an electric current but his experiments failed. Then in 1821 the Frenchman Pierre Berthier discovered deposits of a clay-like material, red and firm. The decomposition product recovered from this rock containing calcium and silicate contained 52% aluminium oxide (Al_2O_3). As this discovery was made near the village of Les Baux-en-Provence in southern France, he called this ore bauxite.

In 1825 the Danish scientist Hans Christian Oersted succeeded in obtaining traces of aluminium by distilling the product of the reaction between a potassium solution (a mixture of potassium and mercury) and aluminium chloride ($AlCl_3$); the residue was a small amount of impure aluminium. Two years later the German chemistry professor Friedrich Wöhler described a method for obtaining aluminium in the form of a grey powder which was based on reducing aluminium chloride by means of a potassium mixture. By using this powder he managed to establish the chemical properties of aluminium. In 1845 he produced – again by reducing aluminium chloride by means of a potassium mixture – round nuggets the size of a pinhead, which then enabled him to determine the physical properties of the metal, its density and hence also one of its unique features – its low weight.

The recovery of larger quantities of aluminium became possible in 1852 when the Frenchman Henry Sainte-Claire Deville – with backing from Emperor Napoleon III – improved on the method used by Wöhler. This involved the reduction of the double chloride of sodium and aluminium and so represented the first commercial method for obtaining aluminium. At that time it was a «precious» metal, more expensive than gold or platinum. At the World Exposition in Paris in 1855 an ingot of aluminium was presented under the title of «silver from clay». The foundation stone for the

Conference Centre and Industrial Theatre,
Foster & Partners, Glasgow, Great Britain

Extension to ING Bank & NNH Headoffices,
(EEA) Erick van Egeraat, Budapest, Hungary

ING Bank & NNH Headoffices,
Mecanoo Budapest,
Budapest, Hungary

production of aluminium on a large scale was laid in 1858 by Henry-Louis Le Chatelier. By 1890 about 200 tonnes of aluminium had been produced with the aid of the method developed by Sainte-Claire Deville. In 1885 the American Hamilton Y. Cassner improved the Deville method such that the annual production of aluminium could climb to 15 tonnes.

The year 1886 saw two young scientists, Paul Toussaint Héroult in France and Charles Martin Hall in the USA, both 23 years old, working separately and each unaware of the work of the other, submit their patents for a method to produce aluminium. Both had discovered that aluminium oxide dissolves in molten cryolite and can then be decomposed by electrolysis by passing a high current through the cryolite bath so that the raw metal starts to melt. This method triggered a veritable «aluminium boom». Even today the economic production of aluminium is based on the Hall-Héroult method, although it has undergone many technical improvements over the years. The first commercial plants for aluminium production by electrolysis appeared in 1888. In Europe the first factory was erected with the help of Héroult at Neuhausen am Rheinfall in Switzerland. In the USA the Aluminium Company of America was founded in Pittsburgh, Pennsylvania; they used the Hall method. In France the Société Electrométallurgique Française in Froges, département Isère, was set up – a factory equipped with the first electrolyte baths in France for the industrial production of aluminium using the electrolysis method.

Between 1887 and 1892 the Austrian Karl-Jozef Bayer, son of the founder of the Bayer Chemicals Company, developed the Bayer method which allowed the large-scale recovery of aluminium oxide from bauxite. Aluminium – thanks to its low weight – has been an important material for the aerospace industry from as early as 1914 – owing to the «demand» generated by World War I (aircraft, airships). And in 1947 the metal was first used in a mass-produced vehicle, the Panhard Dyna. In 1900 the annual production of aluminium was 8000 tonnes; by 1920 this had risen to 128 000 tonnes. Just 26 years later this figure had soared again to 681 000 tonnes. And by 1997 annual output had reached 22 million tonnes. Aluminium is a relatively «young» metal since its production and use only date from 1854. Therefore, it is pointless to compare its «life» with other non-ferrous metals like copper, lead and tin, which have been used for thousands of years. Nevertheless, in terms of tonnes produced, aluminium has in the meantime overtaken those non-ferrous metals (copper: 11.5 million tonnes; lead: 5.4 million tonnes; tin: 200 000 tonnes – 1997 production figures) despite its low weight. Added to the 22 million tonnes recovered directly are another 7 million obtained from recycled material (1997 figures).

Aluminium in building

In 1897 the architect Lorenzo de Rossi specified silvery white aluminium sheets for the covering to the cupola on the San Gioacchino church in Rome. These sheets are still in a very good condition today. Since that time aluminium has been regarded as one of the mainstays of architectural materials, not only because of the artistic or decorative examples of its use, like the Eros statue in Piccadilly Circus, London, an aluminium casting dating from 1893, or the aluminium components of the Empire State Building in New York, built in 1935 (the first building to make use

Ichthus College,
(EEA) Erick van Egeraat,
Rotterdam, Netherlands

Kikutake Architects Office,
Kikutake Architects, Tokyo, Japan

of anodized aluminium), but also because the developments surrounding this «new» material attracted the interest of modern architects. For instance, Laurence Kocher and Albert Frey, who demonstrated an aluminium house at the 1931 architecture exhibition in New York. Their «Aluminaire House» was therefore a direct rival to the Maison Dom-ino of Le Corbusier. For Walter Gropius, founder of the Bauhaus, aluminium was «the material of the future». Following World War II more and more new opportunities appeared for the use of aluminium in architecture.

One good example of this is the aluminium house in colonial style by the architect Jean Prouvé dating from 1949, which opened up the possibilities for the later works of Renzo Piano and Peter Rice. Thanks to its low weight, this house could be transported from France to Niamey in Niger. In 1974 Sir Norman Foster presented a crucial concept in which the facades and roof of the Sainsbury Centre for Visual Arts in Norwich, Great Britain, were covered with a unique module consisting of deep-drawn aluminium panels. Today aluminium – starting with simple window frames – is gradually conquering the complete facade (spandrel panels, cladding, blinds, sunshades, etc.), the roof and loadbearing systems, thus anticipating a single material for the envelope and the structure.

THE PRODUCTION OF ALUMINIUM

From bauxite to aluminium oxide

After oxygen and silicon, aluminium, with 8%, is the third most common element found in the Earth's crust (lithosphere). However, in the natural state it is never found as a pure metal but rather only as a constituent of many minerals in conjunction with silicic acid or oxygen. In the natural state it occurs as aluminium oxide in the mineral bauxite, which also contains titanium, silicon and – imparting its characteristic red colour – iron oxide. This is the only ore which permits the economic extraction of aluminium. In order that bauxite can be exploited economically, it has to exhibit an aluminium oxide content of at least 40%. Some 90% of the world's bauxite deposits are in tropical and subtropical countries. At the moment Australia alone accounts for 30% of global production. Other deposits have been discovered and developed in Guinea,

Jamaica, Guyana, Surinam, Brazil, India and Cameroon. Europe's main mining areas are in Greece, Hungary, France and Yugoslavia. The bauxite deposits developed up to now can cover the needs of several centuries without having to take into account possible further discoveries. Bauxite is mainly obtained from open-cast mines and in the majority of cases processed into aluminium oxide in the country of origin. The aluminium oxide is subsequently sent to dry electrolysis plants in the country or, more frequently, abroad. Four to five tonnes of bauxite are required to produce two tonnes of aluminium oxide, which yield one tonne of aluminium.

In the Bayer process aluminium hydroxide is obtained from bauxite by applying pressure and heat in order to produce aluminium oxide (Al_2O_3) by way of calcination. The bauxite is washed and dissolved in sodium hydroxide in the digester by applying high pressure at a high temperature. The resulting solution is rich in sodium aluminate, and the undissolved bauxite residue contains iron, silicon and titanium. This residue – popularly known as «red mud» – gradually settles on the base of the filter press and is removed. The clear sodium aluminate solution is pumped into a huge tank known as the precipitator. Fine particles of aluminium oxide are added in order to initiate the precipitation as the solution cools. The particles sink to the bottom of the precipitator and are drawn off from there. Subsequent roasting in the rotary kiln at 1100°C drives off the water from the chemical compound. The result is a white powder – pure aluminium oxide. The sodium hydroxide is returned to the start of the process to be used again.

From aluminium oxide to aluminium
The melting point of aluminium oxide is very high (in excess of 2000°C). Therefore, the process begins with dissolving the aluminium oxide in a fused cryolite (Na_3AlF_6), a readily melted natural aluminium-sodium fluoride, at a temperature of about 950°C in a steel cell (or «pot») provided with a carbon or graphite coating. A high amperage, low voltage current (150 000 A) passes from one sacrificial graphite anode (positive) made from petroleum coke and pitch, through the electrolytic cell to a permanent cathode (negative) formed by the carbon or graphite coating on the cell. This current ensures that the solution is broken down into oxygen and aluminium. During this process the oxygen migrates to the graphite electrode immersed in the molten electrolyte and is converted to carbon monoxide or carbon dioxide. At regular intervals a hammer is employed to break a hole in the surface of the solid crust which forms on the surface of the electrolyte. A defined quantity of aluminium oxide is introduced through this hole. The molten aluminium settles on the base of the bath and is siphoned off from here at regular intervals.

This is generally aluminium with a purity of 99.7 % or higher. The remaining 0.3 % consists of small traces of iron, silicon and other elements present in the aluminium oxide and other materials used during production. The liquid aluminium is poured into a crucible and taken to the foundry. Here in a holding furnace (with a capacity of 50 tonnes) it is kept, cleaned, continuously degassed and solidified to form ingots destined for remelting. The «pure» aluminium is frequently, but not always, mixed with, for example, iron, silicon, magnesium, copper, etc. according to the relevant specification for the respective alloy.

The alloys obtained in this way are cast using the semi-continuous casting method with direct cooling to form ingots or cylindrical billets for extrusion or forging, or slabs for rolling. These products are then fabricated in an extrusion plant, rolling mill, etc. to form semi-finished products like, for example, extruded sections, forged components, sheet, foil, wire, etc. An alternative method is continuous casting in which the ingot stage is omitted and the molten metal processed directly into semi-finished products. A modern aluminium foundry may comprise about 300 «pots», giving an annual output of about 125 000 tonnes. However, the newest foundries can reach production figures of 350 000 to 400 000 tonnes. Even though the aluminium is «extracted» at a temperature of 950°C, the melting point of the pure metal is only 660°C. Some foundries exploit this fact in order to add recycled aluminium to the new metal. A comparison of production cycles confirms that the recycled metal only requires 5% of the energy required for producing new aluminium – without there being any differences in the quality or the properties of the new and recycled metals.

CLASSIFICATION OF EXAMPLES

In architecture, we can say that the whole is greater than the sum of the parts, or more accurately, that the overall architectural language of a building influences the assembly of the technological details during the design process. At the same time, the technical options and the properties of the material and the components fabricated from that material determine the language of the finished building by way of the arrangement of the engineering and architectural details. Therefore, it is certainly possible to explain the architectural concept of the building by means of and based on the technological details.

The 25 examples shown in the following are designated with pictograms. These pictograms (max. four per example) enable us to classify the example according to its most important aspects with respect to the use of aluminium. Aluminium and/or its alloys are employed as follows:

1   2   3   4

– 1: For structures or loadbearing elements of a structure; generally, these elements are produced by means of extrusion, the section(s) being chosen to suit the requirements.
– 2: Walls
– 3: Roofs
– 4: Windows and various other frames

South elevation.

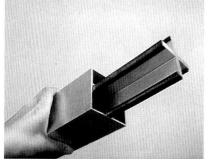

Combination of cruciform column section and square tubular casing.

Living room.

ALUMINIUM HOUSE

Toyo Ito & Associates

Design: This aluminium house is occupied by a married couple and is situated in Tokyo's quiet residential district of Setagaya-ku. The ground floor accommodates kitchen, bedroom and bathroom, while the first floor has an outdoor terrace plus a bedroom with en suite bathroom for guests. The solarium in the middle of the house passes through both floors and allows plenty of daylight to enter the building; it can be ventilated when necessary. It can be opened up to – or closed off from – all the rooms on both floors. The use of aluminium for all the structural members and exposed surfaces underlines the softness of the natural lighting and creates the impression of a calm and harmonious design. Therefore, the special qualities of aluminium soften the obvious differences between the individual structural elements, the partition walls and other details of the construction. The tranquil texture of aluminium, together with the abstract effect which results from the use of lightweight aluminium components, reinforces the impression of the structure «melting into the background». As the columns, like the windows and doors, are integrated in the construction of the partition walls, the structure is no more dominant than the furniture and fittings.

Construction: The use of the structural properties of aluminium enabled the architects to pursue the objective of unity of structure and finishes. This is achieved by employing aluminium for the exposed surfaces, and by combining the diverse application options offered by extruded sections. The extrusion process allows very complex but at the same time highly accurate parts to be very easily fabricated from aluminium. Therefore, the use of this leading

Junction between column and floor construction.

Rubber membranes were installed between roof and walls to dampen vibrations.

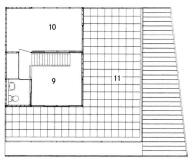

Plan of upper floor.

1 Japanese room
2 Entrance
3 Living room
4 Bathroom
5 Solarium
6 WC
7 Bedroom
8 Kitchen
9 Void
10 Guest room
11 Terrace

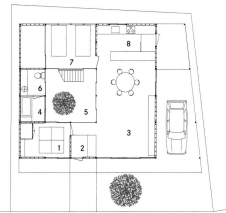

Plan of ground floor.

South and east elevations.

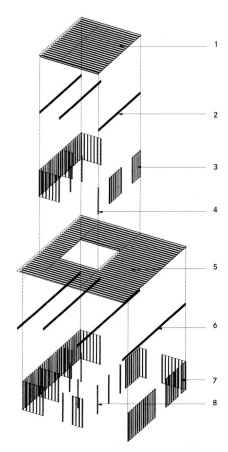

Structural concept showing individual members.
1 Ribbed aluminium plate (RF), plate t = 4 mm,
   rib 96 x 70 x 8 x 9 mm,
   A5083S-H112 AS110A
2 Beam (RF), 96 x 70 x 6 - 6 x 12 mm,
   A6N01S-T5 AS175
3 Ribbed aluminium wall plate,
   A6063S-T5 AS210
4 Column core, 62 x 62 x 7 mm,
   A 7003S-T5 AS210
   Column casing, 70 x 70 x 2 mm,
   A6063S-T5 AS210
5 Ribbed aluminium plate (2F), plate t = 4 mm,
   rib 146 x 70 x 8 x 9 mm,
   A5083S-H112 AS110A
6 Beam (2F), 146 x 70 x 6 - 6 x 15 mm,
   A6N01S-T5 AS210
7 Ribbed aluminium wall plate,
   A6063S-T5 AS210
8 Column core, 62 x 62 x 7 mm,
   A7003S-T5 AS210
   Column casing, 70 x 70 x 2 mm,
   A-6063S-T5 AS210

Canopy, view of I-section beam.

Welding the roof sheeting.

Erecting the door/window frames (which also serve as column casings).

technology would without doubt allow marketing the design and construction of this type of building on a commercial scale. The ribbed aluminium sheets with their smooth appearance, as used for walls, floor and roof, distribute the flow of forces and hence enable the elements to appear very delicate. At 55 kg/m^2 the self-weight of the building is much less than the 1050 kg/m^2 typical for a similar reinforced concrete design. At the same time, the versatility and the durability of aluminium enable it to be used as loadbearing members for the external walls in such a way that the columns can act as frames for the windows. (Extrusion allows column casing and window frame to be combined in one member.)

The construction, which takes up that Japanese tradition of lightness and modular construction, is essentially made up of four different aluminium elements:

– Welded 96 x 70 x 8 x 9 mm sheets (4 mm thick) for the roof covering, 146 x 70 x 8 x 9 mm sheets (4 mm thick) for the upper floor
– Cruciform columns (62 x 62 x 7 mm) inside square hollow sections (70 x 70 x 2 mm)
– 96 x 70 x 6 - 6 x 12 mm I-section beams for roof, 146 x 70 x 6 - 6 x 15 mm for upper floor
– Extruded wall panels 300 mm wide

Sliding aluminium blinds are fitted to all window and door openings.

Materials: The extruded A6063S-T5 AS210 aluminium sheets for the walls are «tray»-type sections with folded edges. These 300 mm elements include three T-section ribs on the inside,

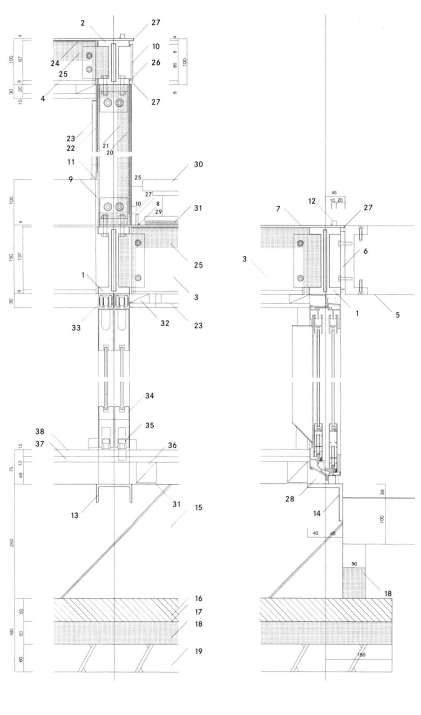

Vertical sections through walls.
1 Beam 146 x 70 x 6 - 6 x 15 mm
2 Beam 96 x 70 x 6 - 6 x 12 mm
3 Rib 146 x 6 x 9 mm
4 Rib 96 x 6 x 9 mm
5 Pergola: aluminium flats, 150 x 15 mm, axis 300 mm
6 Aluminium flat, 125 x 10 mm
7 Ribbed aluminium plate, t = 4 mm, urethane paint finish
8 Aluminium flat, 35 x 5 mm
9 Edge trim, 100 x 6 mm
10 Edge trim, t = 4 mm
11 Aluminium angle, 15 x 15 x 3 mm
12 Flashing, aluminium bar, 10 x 10 mm
13 Horizontal stainless steel channel, 80 x 40 x 5 x 4.5 mm
14 Horizontal stainless steel angle, 80 x 80 x 8 mm
15 Reinforced concrete foundation, t = 250 mm
16 Concrete blinding, t = 50 mm
17 Polyethylene damp-proof membrane
18 Thermal insulation, t = 50 mm
19 Hardcore, t = 60 mm
20 Rubber membrane, t = 3 mm, for vibration control
21 Sprayed phenolic resin, t = 30 mm
22 Butyl rubber seal, t = 5 mm
23 Plasterboard, t = 9 mm, PVC enamel resin paint finish
24 Rubber membrane, t = 3 mm, for vibration control
25 Sprayed phenolic resin, t = 4.5 mm
26 Butyl rubber seal
27 Seal
28 Mortar
29 Weld
30 Precast concrete slab for deck, t = 25 cm
31 Rubber filler, t = 10 mm
32 Timber framing to ceiling, 45 x 20 mm
33 Track for sliding door, 34 x 31 mm
34 Glass door: spruce frame, t = 32 mm
35 Track for sliding doors
36 Floor joist, 45 x 45 mm
37 Plywood backing, t = 12 mm
38 Flooring, t = 15 mm

Horizontal section through walls.
1 Wall framing members: aluminium, w = 300 mm
2 Wall edge trim: aluminium, w = 190 mm
3 Column core: aluminium, 62 x 62 x 7 mm
4 Column casing (sash frame): aluminium, 70 x 70 x 2 + 70 x 15 mm
5 Sprayed urethane finish, t = 30 mm
6 Plasterboard: t = 12.5 mm, PVC enamel resin paint finish
7 Aluminium door
8 Prefabricated sash, double sliding
9 Aluminium angle, 20 x 20 x 3 mm
10 Butyl rubber membrane, t = 2 mm
11 Neoprene rubber packing
12 Neoprene rubber membrane, t = 3 mm
13 Neoprene rubber membrane, t = 5 mm
14 Seal

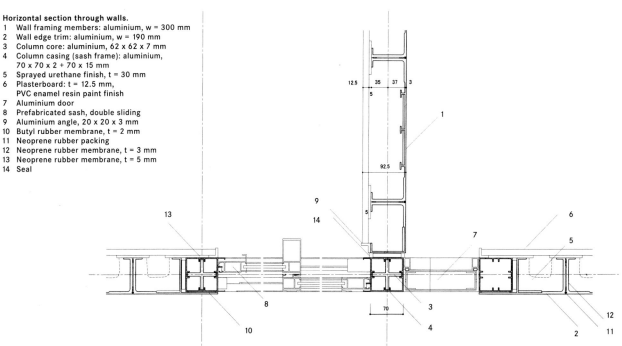

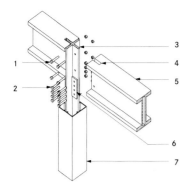

Column beam junction.
1 Stainless steel bolts, 2 No. M6
2 Stainless steel bolts, 4 No. M6
3 Column core, 62 x 62 x 7 mm
4 Cut-out
5 Beam, 146 x 70 x 6 - 6 x 15 mm
6 Beam bracket: flat bar,
  90 x 23.5 x 4 mm
7 Column casing, 70 x 70 x 2 mm

View of underside of solarium roof.

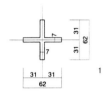

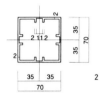

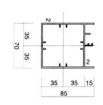

Details of various aluminium components.
1 Column core, 62 x 62 x 7 mm, A7003S-T5
2 Column casing (sash frame),
  70 x 70 x 2 mm, A 6063S-T5
3 Wall framing members, w = 300, A6063S-T5
4 Beam (2F), 146 x 70 x 6 - 6 x 15 mm, A6N01S-T5
5 Rib (2F), 146 x 70 x 6 x 9 mm, A5083S-H112

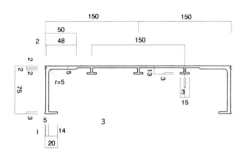

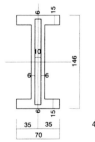

produced integrally with the element by means of extrusion. These three small Tees serve to stiffen the element and to attach the rubber membranes needed to dampen vibrations. The outer panels were given a polyurethane layer as thermal insulation. The connections between the individual panels are sealed by means of neoprene membranes and gaskets. Protection to the panels is by means of PVC resin paint outside and a sprayed phenolic resin paint inside. The inner faces of the panels have diverse finishes: panels ready to paint, or wood. The A5083S-H112 AS 110A aluminium sheets for the roof covering have been given a urethane paint finish.

Address: Sakurajosui, Setagaya-ku, Tokyo, Japan
Architect: Toyo Ito & Associates
Client: Private individual
Consulting engineers: Oak Structural Design Office (structure);
                  Kawaguchi Mechanical Engineering (services)
Construction period: 1997-2000
Aluminium components: welded ribbed sheets for upper floor and roof:
aluminium A5083S-H112 AS110A;   beams: aluminium A6N01S-T5 AS175;
                  wall cladding, extruded stiffening panels, column casings:
aluminium A6063S-T5 AS210;   columns: aluminium A7003S-T5 AS210
Fabricators: Sky Aluminium Company (welded aluminium ribbed sheets);
Showa Aluminium Corporation (extruded aluminium components)

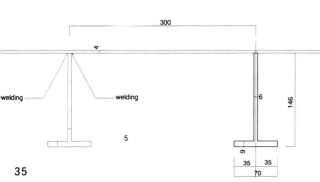

East elevation at night.

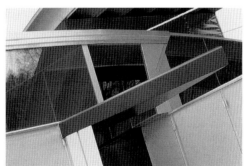

Detail of entrance.

East elevation.

View of the interior.

All elements contribute to the sequence of fluid transitions in the interior.

KÖNIGSEDER HOUSE

Helmut Richter

Design: The detached house of a doctor in a small town near Linz in Austria formed the starting point for this project. According to the plan, the new annex was to contain out-patient treatment rooms and a pharmacy for the general medical practitioner. Retention of the mural on the eastern facade of the existing house also formed part of the architect's brief. These now decorate the waiting room. The very expressive architecture of the new building stands in juxtaposition to, yet is integrated with, the calm, modest atmosphere of the simple original building. The highly extrovert form ensues from the loadbearing construction and the textures of the various facades. The entrance to the out-patients section is located at the transition between old and new construction. The link between foyer and waiting room is a sequence of fluid transitions between ever-changing spatial impressions, brought about by the embracing effect of the various lines and curves and accentuated by views of the external surroundings, the incoming daylight as well as the design and positioning of furniture, which further punctuates the setting. The interplay of the architectural elements employed, like inclined windows, the vaulting of the roof, huge mirrors, colours and dominating lighting effects, both artificial and natural, creates a very complex sequence of spatial impressions. The long hallway conducts the patient from the entrance – leaving behind the pharmacy – to the reception; from there the patient is guided along the reception desk and into the waiting room. All the details, from the positioning of radiators to the rhythm of the plywood panels to the lines of lighting units, reinforce the orientation of the interior: the patient is steered directly to the doctor in his surgery.

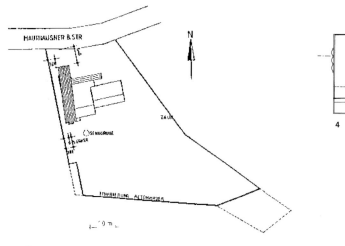

Site plan.

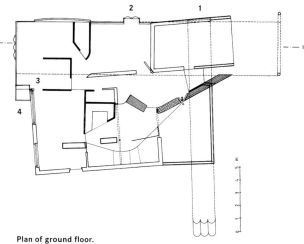

Plan of ground floor.

Section.

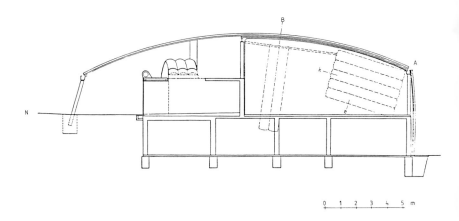

Fixing of Para shells to corrugated sheeting.

Construction: Two parabolic shells arranged at 90° to each other create a long-span construction which encloses the existing building on the north and east sides and in so doing forms a new approach to the house and the out-patients section by means of welcoming canopies. Looked at from the road, the loadbearing construction (raking columns) to the aluminium shell punctuates the approach and expresses symbolically the structural principle. The garage is placed beneath the upper shell; the lower shell slips under this cantilever. A cladding of red fabric creates the link between the two shells. Timber framing is used for the non-loadbearing walls, which are clad in okoumé plywood.

Materials: Aluminium determines the character of the annex. The corrugated profiles and the shells, curving along their longitudinal axes, establish two different rhythms for the facade. The «horizontal» shells initiate a dynamic progression, while the upper, vertical shells represent a contrapuntal departure. The elements of the Para building system were, so to speak, «recycled» for this domestic application. The Para shells, loadbearing designs with low self-weight, were developed by the engineer F. Ragailler. These are in the form of an arc with a primary radius of 21 m and secondary radius of 325 mm. Originally intended for the roofs of aircraft hangars (they can carry loads of up to 2.5 kN/m^2 on spans of 22–28 m), were utilized here owing to their loadbearing capacity, but primarily because of their expressive language.

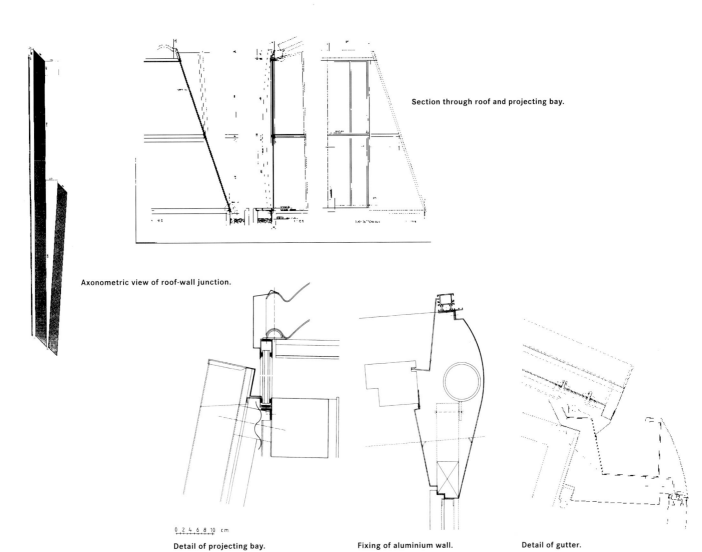

Section through roof and projecting bay.

Axonometric view of roof-wall junction.

0 2 4 6 8 10 cm

Detail of projecting bay.

Fixing of aluminium wall.

Detail of gutter.

Connection between Para shell and corrugated sheeting.

Address: Baumgartenberg, Machland, Austria
Architect: Helmut Richter
Client: Private individual
Construction period: 1977-80
Aluminium components: Para-Systembau, longitudinal radius 21 m,
transverse radius 0.325 m, camber 137 mm, width of shell element: 610 mm;
twin-leaf shell with thermal transmittance $U = 0.46$ W/m^{2}K
Fabricator: Para

General view of new annex.

North elevation.

View of entrance and main terrace. Aluminium was also used for the new window opposite the bathroom. The photo was taken during construction.

ANNEX FOR ZITA KERN

ARTEC Architekten

Design: This project is located in the Marchfeld region, near the eastern suburbs of Vienna. Set amid an ensemble of agricultural buildings, the particular geometry of the aluminium sections of this extension form a contrast to the variegated roofscape of the old farm. The owner, Zita Kern, not only manages the farm, she also carries out literary research. Therefore, the aim of the project was to add a spacious study to the building. In addition, the original facilities were to be extended by adding a large bathroom, a boiler room, a store and, most importantly, an entrance hall. The owner's wish was for the study to be set apart from the agricultural surroundings, and the architects favoured using an old cowshed. The building was much in need of renovation and the roof had to be removed as it was in danger of collapsing. The masonry walls also showed signs of considerable settlement. Now the project is complete, the new rooms are partly screened by the old walls which were retained to form the foundation for the new architecture. The study is located on the first floor. Although this part is linked to the farmyard, it is at the same time separated from it. The intellectual domain is detached in a simple manner from the world of labour. The space enclosed by the new roof construction can be divided by a movable partition, while the roof construction itself exhibits a «crystalline» geometry which represents a complete departure from the surrounding roofscape. It has two shallow, opposing pitches spanning in the most economic direction. There are two abruptly intersecting pitched sections on the south and south-east sides. The stair which leads to the new part of the building is quite clearly a separate entity. It is placed on the outside of the existing building and links the new section with the farmyard.

The rough with the smooth, the soil with the sky.

Roof-wall junction: polished aluminium sheets
for the wall cladding, trapezoidal profile sheeting for
the roof covering.

The bathroom is situated between existing walls on the ground floor. Light enters through a long band of glass in the roof on which up to 20 mm of rainwater can accumulate in order to modify the incoming daylight by way of reflection and refraction. Access to the two terraces with their wooden floors is via sliding and hinged doors. The terraces integrate the new roof in the old building and extend the study to the outside, thereby adopting a typically urban relationship here among rural surroundings. Boiler room and store are located on the ground floor.

Construction: The masonry walls have been retained in the chosen solution. These are only strengthened with reinforced concrete, anchorages or spandrel panels at the ends as required. Two floors were erected on this base. One is of reinforced concrete and forms the roof to the bathroom as well as the covered entrance porch and supporting construction for the large terrace. In addition, it links the old timber beams below. The other floor, which cantilevers out on the south side (over the stairs), rests on a new timber beam on the IPN sections of the old vaulted brick ceiling to the cowshed, carrying the load of the study. The new roof construction is supported by timber beams.

Materials: The external cladding employs 8 mm thick poplar plywood boards to which vertical battens are attached, thereby forming a ventilation cavity. Polished aluminium sheets 2 mm thick are screwed to these battens. The weight of the standard size (1500 x 3000 mm) aluminium sheets meant they could be easily erected by just two workers. All aluminium components, rectangular sheets or trapezoidal profile sheeting, window frames and chimney are made from polished aluminium without any further finishes. This polished aluminium reflects the changing colours of the sky and the seasons. Natural-colour anodized 2 mm aluminium sheets are used for wall and interior finishes (bathroom, shower, sliding door tracks, etc.). The aluminium hinged and sliding doors belong to the Alusuisse system.

Address: Pysdorf 1, Raasdorf, Austria
Architect: ARTEC Architekten –
                 Bettina Götz, Richard Manahl, Maria Kirchweger (assistant)
Client: Zita Kern, Raasdorf
Structural engineer: Oskar Graf, Vienna
Construction period: 1997-98
Aluminium components: external and internal cladding: plain sheets and trapezoidal profile sheeting: Alusuisse; doors: Alusuisse system
Fabricator: Alusuisse

View through the «Antisun» solar-control glass towards the main terrace.

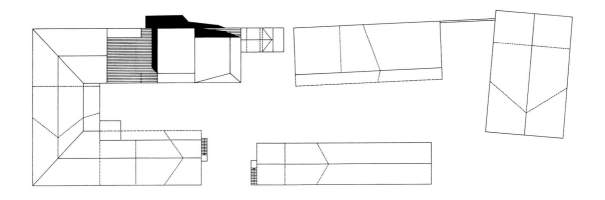

Site layout.

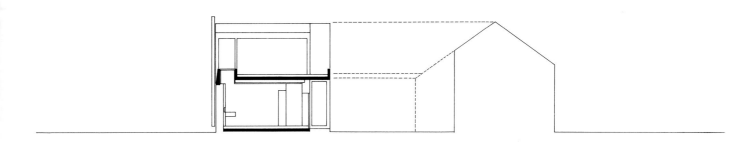

Section through bathroom and main terrace.

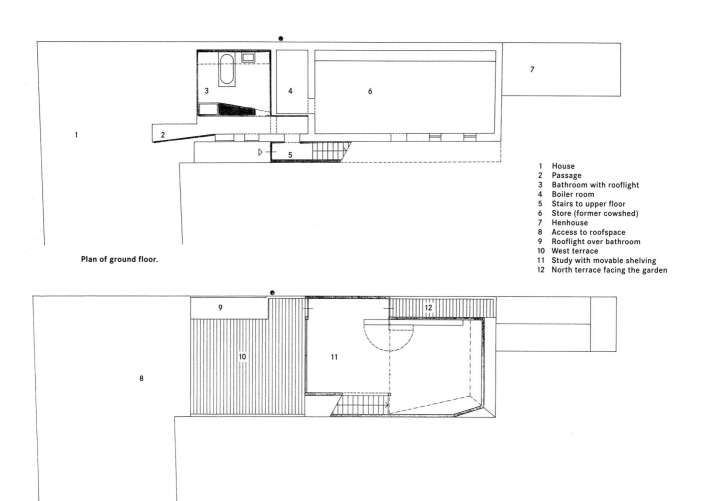

Plan of ground floor.

1 House
2 Passage
3 Bathroom with rooflight
4 Boiler room
5 Stairs to upper floor
6 Store (former cowshed)
7 Henhouse
8 Access to roofspace
9 Rooflight over bathroom
10 West terrace
11 Study with movable shelving
12 North terrace facing the garden

Plan of upper floor.

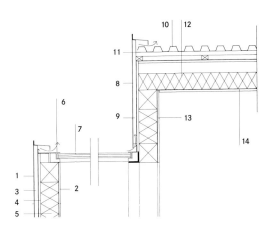

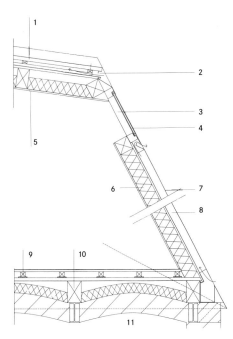

Junction between roof and «Antisun» solar-control glass over stairs.
1   Aluminium cladding
2   Poplar plywood
3   Cavity
4   Wood fibre board
5   Timber frame
6   Aluminium cover
7   Solar-control glass (Parsol® green)
8   Aluminium cladding
9   Cavity
10 Aluminium trapezoidal profile sheeting
11 Wood fibre board
12 Timber frame
13 Poplar plywood
14 Poplar plywood

Section through east end of building. Junction between existing building (masonry walls, brick arch floor) with new annex (timber frame, aluminium cladding: plain aluminium sheets for walls, trapezoidal profile sheeting for roof).
1   Aluminium trapezoidal profile sheeting
2   Cavity
3   Timber frame
4   Solar-control glass (Parsol® green)
5   Wood fibre board
6   Poplar plywood
7   Aluminium cladding
8   Cavity
9   Timber frame
10 New timber frame
11 Old brick arch floor

Rooflight for illuminating and ventilating bathroom.
1   Aluminium cover
2   Poplar plywood
3   Poplar plywood
4   Ventilation flap
5   Mirror
6   Rubber covering
7   Aluminium cladding
8   Timber grating (larch wood)
9   New reinforced concrete slab
10 Old timber construction (dowelled timber beams)
11 Poplar plywood

Bathroom interior.

General view.

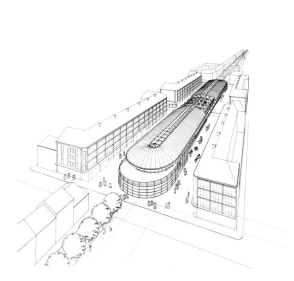

Perspective view looking from the south. The brasserie terrace in the foreground overlooks avenue de la République.

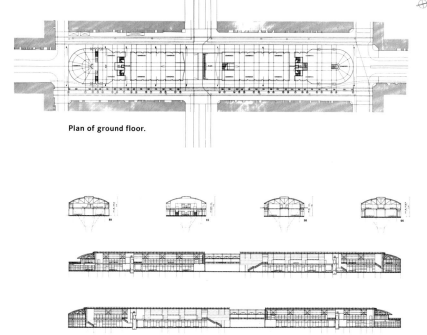

Plan of ground floor.

Longitudinal and cross sections.

46

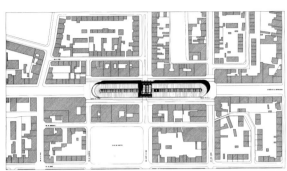

Location plan. The shape of «Le Paquebot» fits
beautifully into the town centre.

COMMERCIAL CENTRE – LE PAQUEBOT

Claude Vasconi

Design: This building, resembling the form of a steamship
(French: «paquebot»), is located on a widened section of avenue de
la République between rue de Stalingrad and rue Jean Jaurès in
Sainte-Nazaire, famous for its shipyards, on France's Atlantic coast.
The town was totally destroyed in 1944 but was rebuilt during the
1950s. The building with its armoured shell so to speak, which was
erected as part of a larger town centre redevelopment programme,
is 230 m long. It houses shops, offices, a multipurpose hall and
facilities for leisure activities (e.g. bowling alley). The acknowl-
edged objective of the project is to revitalize retail trade, encour-
aging it to return to the town centre and reverse the tendency to
migrate to the suburbs. The complex consists of two blocks united
by the outline and construction of the roof. A public square at the
junction of rue Albert de Mun and avenue de la République separates the two blocks. This square is framed at upper floor level by
footbridges which assure the optical continuity of the building form.
The entire ground floor is occupied by shops open only to the street
on the west and east elevations. Both ends of Le Paquebot are
semicircular, rounding off the building, so to speak, and facilitating
the passage of buses. The first floor is reached by way of a central
stair at place Albert de Mun, which leads to the footbridges and
offices, as well as via stairs and lifts located in the passages
running across the building. The southern semicircular end to the
building accommodates a bar/brasserie with outdoor terrace on the
first floor which can also be reached from the ground floor and the
multipurpose hall. In the northern block the central passage is lined
by offices. This passage splits into two outer walkways which then
lead to the footbridges at place Albert de Mun.

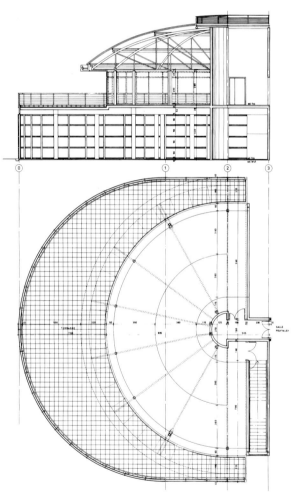

Side elevation and plan of terrace.

Construction: All the exposed loadbearing structure consists of metal circular hollow sections. The bowstring roof trusses are supported on a double colonnade of metal square hollow sections (height 3.35 m) spaced 19.80 m apart, with three different longitudinal spacings: 7.20, 3.60 and 5.40 m. The roof trusses and the purlins consist of circular hollow sections. The circular columns of the ground floor are 3.85 m high and utilize the same longitudinal grid. However, the transverse spacings are 7.20, 5.40 and 7.20 m in order to carry the first floor beams at 800 mm centre to centre.

Materials: The desire to create a large enclosed space and at the same time generate an appearance characterized by lightness and transparency led to a 100% aluminium construction. The distinguishing element of Le Paquebot is its roof covering of natural-colour (i.e. light grey) anodized aluminium, which engages in an interesting dialogue with the dark grey of the neighbouring slate roofs. These aluminium sheets with their radius of 13 m were pre-curved during fabrication and delivered to site in this form. The roof construction comprises aluminium sheeting and thermal insulation on a protective sheathing with a ventilation gap in between. This design also ensures a certain degree of sound insulation against the drumming of rain and hail. The passages inside the building are provided with natural light by way of a vaulted glass roof positioned above the natural ventilation and smoke vents. The first floor is clad in aluminium sandwich panels as a continuation of the roof covering. The material and colour (together with the metal spandrel panels to footbridges and balconies) give roof and first

The aluminium roof covering engages in a dialogue with the surrounding slate roofs.

Interior view of place Albert de Mun; roof trusses of circular hollow sections, aluminium sandwich panel cladding.

floor a uniform appearance. The ceilings to the passages are also clad in aluminium. The setback ground floor gives the impression of it acting as a plinth for the first floor. The floor coverings inside the building represent an extension to the pedestrian areas and passages.

Address: avenue de la République, Saint-Nazaire, France
Architect: Claude Vasconi;   Radu Vincenz, François Maignan (project assistants)
Client: Saint-Nazaire Municipal Authority, G3I, Socafim Ouest; Sonadev (project management)
Structural engineer: Léon Petroff
Inspection: Socotec
Construction period: 1987-89
Aluminium components: aluminium sheets for roof covering, natural-colour anodized aluminium as covering, aluminium sandwich panels for the cladding, frames
Fabricator: Durand Structure (facades and sheet metalworking)

View of the interior.

MABEG HEADQUARTERS

Nicholas Grimshaw & Partners

Design: This office block is situated in the grounds of the MABEG company on an industrial estate parallel to the B 475 trunk road to the south-east of Soest in northern Germany. The MABEG company produces street furniture, information systems and signalling. The international reputation of the company is founded on its consistent dedication to precision, customer care and innovation. Therefore, the complex is intended to reflect this attention to quality which has resulted from MABEG's long-standing collaboration with eminent designers. As the building is intended to serve as a focal point on a site which has in the past been neglected owing to a lack of definitive planning, its appearance must present a certain expressiveness and awaken the idea of permanence. Furthermore, it should at the same time become a sort of trademark of the company in the eyes of the media. The client called for open, friendly and bright working conditions, where possible using daylight. The first feasibility study revealed not only the need for an administration building and exhibition facility, but also the need for a complete rethink of the development process. Therefore, this building satisfies all important tasks: management, sales, marketing and distribution. In addition, there are rooms for meetings and exhibitions. Surrounded by, in terms of design, rather simple production buildings, the MABEG Office Box through its height alone has become the central reference point and unifying element on the site. Raising the building clear of the ground offers both functional and aesthetic advantages. The covered area beneath the first floor can be used for manoeuvring and parking vehicles, in particular delivery vehicles, thereby saving valuable space on this really quite small site. This parking zone can be

View of the exterior.

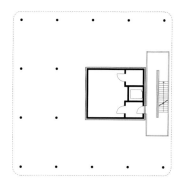

Plan of ground floor.

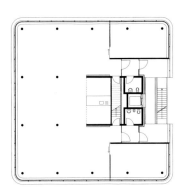

Plan of first floor.

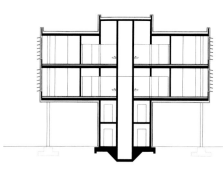

North-south section.

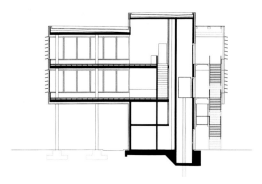

East-west section.

illuminated with the aid of four red warning lamps mounted at each corner on the underside of the first floor. Visitors are treated to a view of the entire industrial estate from the aluminium stairs. Access to the two floors is via this core, painted in the MABEG corporate colour blue.

Construction: The MABEG Office Box makes use of concrete and metal elements. The columns are positioned on a 6 m grid in the north-south direction and 4.5 m in the east-west direction. This latter dimension was selected so that vehicles could pass through. The first floor supported by the circular reinforced concrete columns is positioned at a height of 5 m. Storey heights above this are 3.5 m, giving a clear internal headroom of 3 m. The service core consists of reinforced concrete walls 200 mm thick and completes the loadbearing structure of the building.

Materials: The facade is clad with silver (RAL 9006) 18/76 mm corrugated aluminium sheeting (curved sheets for the corners of the building) fixed to vertical aluminium rails (100 x 50 x 5 mm) and interrupted by horizontal window bands 2.6 m high behind perforated aluminium sunshades. The loadbearing walls of 120 mm thick reinforced concrete also include 100 mm thick thermal insulation. The sunshades to the corner windows were designed and fabricated especially for this project. They consist of sections in the shape of a quarter-circle. The fair-face concrete of the floors is partly clad with white, perforated plasterboard, thereby improving the acoustics in the various office and exhibition areas. The grey carpet also helps to cut noise, while in the kitchen and circulation zones a black rubber floor covering has been used. The external stairs covered by a glass roof are made from aluminium sections from the «machine» range. The bottom flight can be raised like a drawbridge with the help of a simple cable mechanism in order to prevent unauthorized persons gaining access to the building when it is not occupied.

Address: Soest, Germany
Architects: Nicholas Grimshaw & Partners Ltd;
Nicholas Grimshaw and Michael Pross (Berlin); Thomas Deuble, Helle Schröder (design team)
Client: MABEG-Kreuschner GmbH & Co. KG
Structural engineers: Specht, Kalleja & Partner, Berlin
Interior fittings: Kühn Bauer Partner, Berlin/Munich
Acoustics and building science: Bauphysik Müller BBM, Berlin
Construction period: 1996-99
Aluminium components: 18 x 76 mm corrugated aluminium sheeting
Aluminium sunshades: extruded sections; external form: curved with a radius of 200 mm
and a camber of radius 15 mm, 4 mm thick
Fabricator: Spagnol Luthi Associés SA, Renens, Switzerland;
Pechiney (erection of aluminium facade and sunshades)

The radiator grille of a truck was the inspiration behind the unconventional facade cladding.

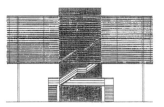

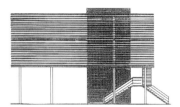

A large-scale model of one corner helped to design the details.

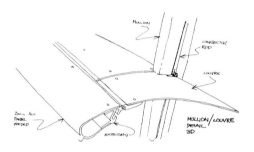

Perspective view of sunshade, variation 1.

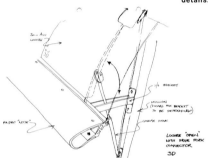

Perspective view of movable sunshade (open), variation 1.

Section through aluminium stair t

Section through head of window.
1   Aluminium flat, 50 x 5 mm
2   Waterproof membrane
3   2 mm aluminium sheet
4   2 mm aluminium sheet, RAL 90
5   Half-round head self-tapping sc
6   Aluminium angle, 30 x 30 x 3-8
7   Aluminium angle, 65 x 15 x 2 m
    plug-welded to perforated alum
8   12 mm dia. stainless steel tie r
    (only at the corners of the buil
9   Aluminium flat, 50 x 5 mm
10 Plastic strip, 50 x 50 x 2 mm
11 Aluminium angle, 70 x 50 x 5 m
12 12 mm dia. stainless steel tie r
    (only at the corners of the buil
13 Hexagonal nuts, M10-0.5d
14 Stainless steel threaded sleeve
    machine screw to DIN 913, OD

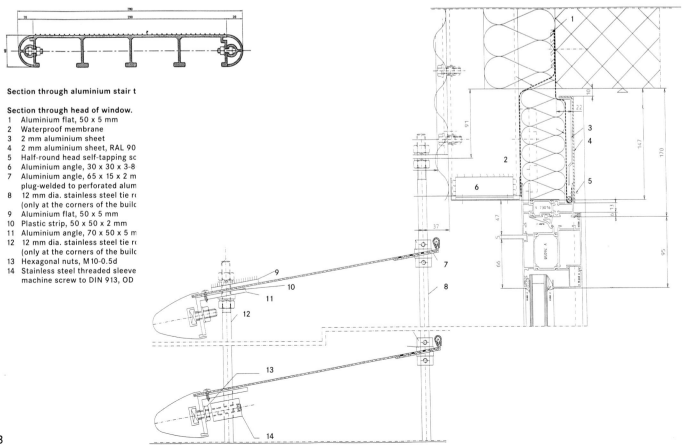

View from the road.

The river in the evening light.

MURA-NO TERRACE

Makoto Sei Watanabe

Design: This information centre and café with a floor area of 389 m² is located on the edge of the small village of Sakauchi among the central uplands of Honshu in the heart of Japan. For the 750 inhabitants and their visitors this centre serves as a meeting place, small concert hall and grocery store. In an authentic natural environment where the future is not being ignored, the architecture of this building emphasizes the naturalness of the river, with its easy fishing in the clear waters, and of the green hills stretching across the horizon. The concept evolved here does not leave nature to itself but rather accentuates its beauty through the insertion of artificial objects. Extending out to the river is a metal jetty from where visitors can enjoy a panoramic view through 300°. Directly alongside there is a large canopy which offers protection from rain and snow (which in this region can be up to 3 m deep). This union of architecture, landscape, art and the natural surroundings fuses into one unique broad space. The facade facing the road is a combination of surfaces whose simplicity is such that they can also be fully appreciated by the occupants of vehicles passing at high speed. The facade facing the river opens out to greet visitors. The walls and roofs of the building lie in different planes, one over the other, playing with the light and the shadows. In the «Wave Garden» poles of carbon fibre are grouped to form a bouquet of light-emitting diodes and solar batteries.

Construction and materials: The exterior utilizes inexpensive, thermally insulated, plain aluminium sandwich panels. Such panels are normally reserved for simple box-type buildings like factories or warehouses. However, in this design the numerous

The concept evolved here does not leave nature to itself but rather accentuates its beauty through the insertion of artificial objects.

planes of the walls meet at diverse angles, acutely or with overlapping edges. These very carefully constructed details also required the fabricator to exercise an equal amount of care during production.

Address: Ibi-Gun, Gifu, Japan
Architects: Makoto Sei Watanabe Architects
Client: Sakauchi-Mura Local Authority, Gifu
Construction period: 1994-95
Aluminium components: thermally insulated aluminium sandwich panels
Fabricator: Hunter Douglas Japan

View of the interior.

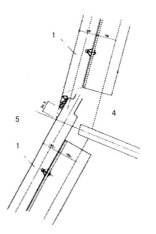

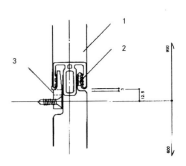

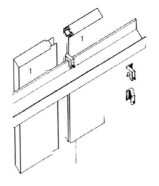

Detail of fixing of aluminium sandwich panels.
1 Thermally insulated aluminium sandwich panel
2 Sealed joint
3 S-shaped clamp
4 Inside
5 Outside

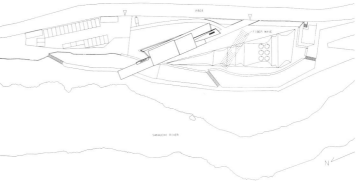

Site layout.

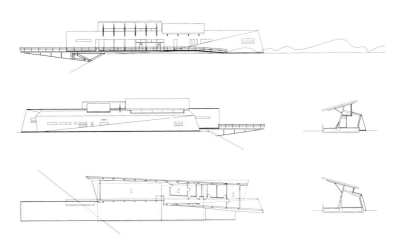

East and west facades, sections.

overall concept. The aluminium (and stainless steel) panels for the external cladding are very large and make use of drained joints. After attaching the panels with a joint width of 3 mm, the resulting three-dimensional bodies were installed. The cladding makes use of panels with four different surface finishes: reflective surfaces, gold-coloured stainless steel surfaces, aluminium with fluorite or aluminium-coloured coating.   The cores of these panels consist of an aluminium honeycomb structure which keeps the panels flat and rigid. The interior makes use of a new material called «Acry honeycomb». The sandwich panels comprise two acrylic glass layers bonded to an aluminium honeycomb structure in the middle. The light passes through this honeycomb structure to illuminate both the interior and the panels themselves. Therefore, this semi-transparent material reveals the inside of the «body of the architecture», e.g. the aluminium honeycomb structure. This technique has helped to realize one of the most important concepts for the architecture of this museum: rendering the invisible visible. Composite panels of aluminium and plastic, also used for some of the walls, form the transition between the transparent and the opaque for the interior. The volume with the curved surface consists of plastics reinforced with semi-transparent fibres (FRP). The floor coverings inside the museum make use of thick plates of galvanized steel which are normally used as a temporary floor covering in industrial situations.

View of the interior.

Address: Tokyo, Japan
Architects: Makoto Sei Watanabe Architect's Office
Client: The Bureau of Port and Harbour; Tokyo Metropolitan Government,
        Tokyo Waterfront Development Inc.
Construction period: 1995-96
Aluminium components: external cladding of aluminium sandwich panels with honeycomb structure, internal cladding of aluminium sandwich panels
(«Acry honeycomb») composite panels of aluminium and plastic
Fabricators: pla-metal PW, Polycolor Industry Co Ltd (internal panels); Shinko-North Co. (external panels: aluminium panels with aluminium honeycomb structure/stainless steel panels with aluminium honeycomb structure)

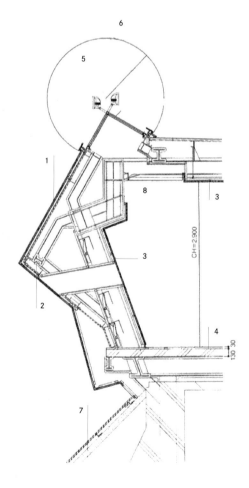

Section through envelope.
1   29 mm aluminium panels with honeycomb structure
     (silver-coloured section)
     27 mm stainless steel panels with honeycomb structure
     (mirror-finish surfaces and gold-coloured section)
2   Mineral wool
3   27 mm acrylic glass panels with honeycomb structure
     (transparent section)
     27 mm aluminium/plastic panels
     (silver-coloured section)
4   7.2 mm galvanized steel plate, parallel form
5   Acrylic glass panel
6   Carbon fibre-reinforced plastic (CFRP)
     (random contours in some places)
7   30 mm granite (flat section)
     Ceramic tiles, random contours (undulating section)
8   Steel open grid, 3.2 dia. x 50 x 50 mm

Detail. The changing daylight alters the way we perceive the building.

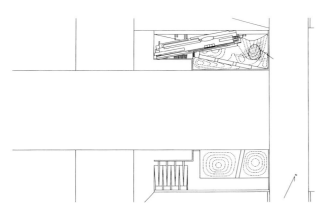

Site layout.

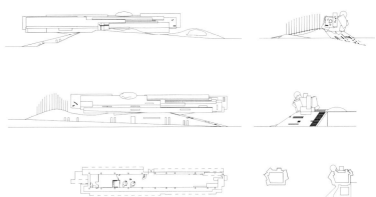

South, east, north and west elevations; plan and sections.

View of the west facade.

The new building engages in a dialogue with the
Art Nouveau style of the old hospital.

The perforated aluminium cladding of the
new extension can be closed to present a
completely unbroken white facade.

Close-up of the pivoting elements of the new extension in the open position.

ENT CLINIC

Ernst Giselbrecht

Design: The extension to the otorhinolaryngology (ear, nose and throat) clinic in Graz set out to achieve two objectives simultaneously: to establish a harmonious link with the existing hospital building and its outstanding Art Nouveau facade, and to instil a calm and reassuring atmosphere for those using the hospital. This is a two-storey construction clad entirely in white aluminium panels. A subtle dialogue ensues between this relatively neutral facade treatment and the decorative facade of the old hospital building. The white finish is a functional and symbolic response to the requirements of hospital care tailored to the needs of people. The ground floor accommodates the reception as well as two areas for special clinical examinations, while the operating theatres are housed on the first floor. Special attention was given to the interior, where natural and welcoming illumination is important. This is especially so in the entrance and in the waiting rooms so that the apprehension which patients can experience upon entering a hospital is quickly alleviated. Furthermore, links with nature and the outside world are established. The rigorous geometry which prevails in the interior layout as well as the combination of materials and components contribute to an atmosphere which communicates care and relaxation, and also tries to convey the impression that the patient's stay in hospital is only temporary and of short duration.

Construction: The structure is supported by concrete columns (390 x 450 mm) on a grid measuring 8 x 8 m and 8 x 4 m, and by walls 150 mm thick. The 300 mm thick reinforced concrete floor slabs are carried on beams 540 mm deep positioned on the

The white-painted aluminium sheeting and glass curtain wall from Schüco.

Plan of ground floor.

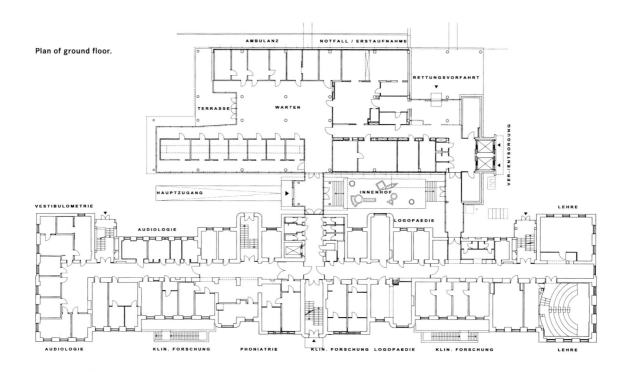

North-west elevation.

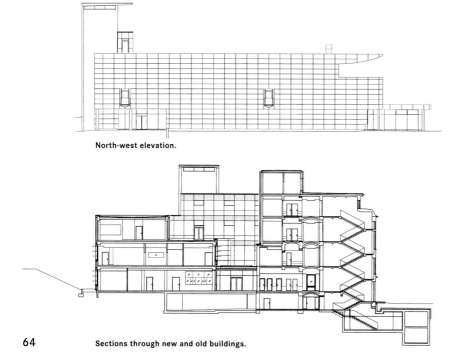

Sections through new and old buildings.

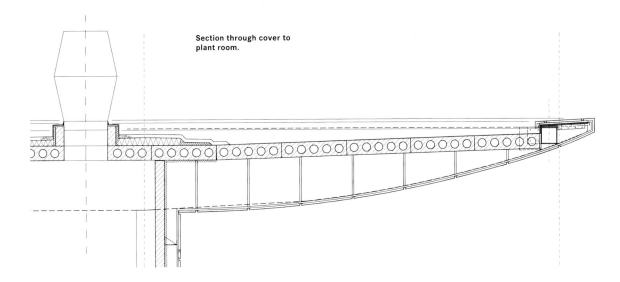

Section through cover to
plant room.

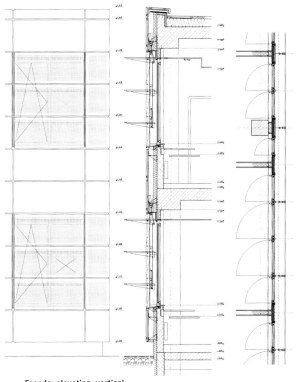

Facade: elevation, vertical
and horizontal sections.

grid lines. The external walls are clad with 90 mm thick thermal insulation and white aluminium panels carried by brackets at each vertical joint.

Materials: The facades are clad with white aluminium sheeting or opaque laminated safety glass. Perforated aluminium sheets, which can be positioned horizontally and vertically for opening and closing, are used in front of the windows. Therefore, the building can be completely closed, for example, in the operating theatre section or to regulate the internal climate in other parts of the extension. Both the construction for the curtain walls and the window frames are made from aluminium sections.

Address: Graz, Austria
Architect: Ernst Giselbrecht with
Kuno Kelih, Johannes Eisenberger, Andreas Moser, Anton Oitzinger, Sandra Gruber, Peter Müller, Andreas Ganzera, Wolfgang Öhlinger (project team)
Client: Steiermärkische Krankenanstalten GesmbH
Consulting engineers: Dr. Friedl/Dr. Rinderer (structure);
Rauterer consultants (electrical services); Wagner consultants (HVAC)
Construction period: 1994-99
Aluminium components: cladding of white aluminium panels, sunshades of perforated aluminium, supporting construction for glass curtain wall, aluminium window frames
Fabricator: Schüco sections (glass curtain wall, window frames)

View of the interior. Perforated
aluminium sheets provide partial
shade for the windows with their
aluminium frames.

Overall view of the complex.

Looking upwards from the
internal forecourt.

The structural glazing: the aluminium sandwich panels and the double glazing form a flush surface.

The side of the building.

LEVI'S GENERAL EUROPEAN HEADQUARTERS

Samyn & Partners

Design: This office complex is located on an industrial estate in the proximity of the campus of Brussels University adjacent the Brussels-Luxembourg railway line. It houses laboratories and the local management, and is divided into two closely related blocks – one rectangular, and the other semicircular and raised clear of the ground on columns. The rectangular block is positioned parallel to the road alongside the railway line; the semicircular block follows the curve of the road. These two blocks are linked by an integral forecourt which steers visitors towards the main entrance, positioned in the centre of the rectangular block. The two vertical access towers, containing stairs and lifts, to the left and the right form the links between the two blocks. The lifts provide users with a view of the forecourt and are protected against unfavourable climatic conditions by a facade equipped with a glass louvre sunshade arrangement. Offices and communication zones are located on the eight floors. The layout of the offices is based on a 1.2 m grid. Cavity floors provide for great flexibility in laying cables and piped services. The character of the building ensues from the contrast between the hypermodern minimalism of the architecture and the high-tech design of the entire complex.

Construction: The facade is made up of horizontal bands alternating between glazing and anodized aluminium sandwich panels. The structural glazing using the Siltal system fixes both the double glazing as well as the aluminium panels without recourse to projecting sections. The aluminium sandwich panels and the double glazing present a completely flat exterior, with neither projections nor recesses. The glazing elements which open are also

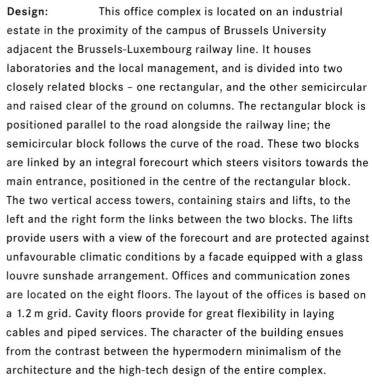

Main elevation and access to the forecourt within the complex.

Main elevation.

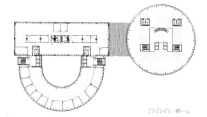

Plan of upper floor.

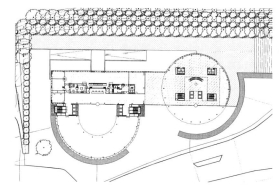

Plan of ground floor.

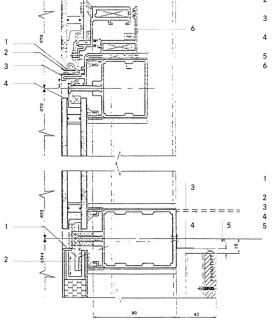

Facade sections.

1 Sil 60 x 15 mm
2 Stainless steel L = 60 mm, axis at 120 mm
3 Bevelled joint over a length of 70 mm for drainage
4 CLO/F (2 mm stainless steel), axis 150 mm
5 Siltal stop
6 Square-socket screw, stainless steel

1 Scaffold clamp fitting, CL large, axis 100 mm
2 Neoprene 3 mm
3 Ventilation and radiator cover
4 Aluminium sheet, 0.7 x 15 x 42 mm
5 Variable level ± 20 mm

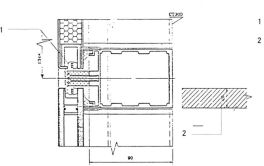

1 CL aluminium, 6 mm, axis 200 mm
2 floor

Detail of corner.

1 Angle clamp (4 mm stainless steel), axis 170 mm
2 Pin, 6 mm, DIN 7
3 Sealing cord of black silicone
4 U95
5 6 mm steel flat
6 Edge of concrete

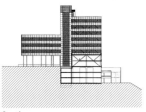

Section.

The integral forecourt.

The complex at night.

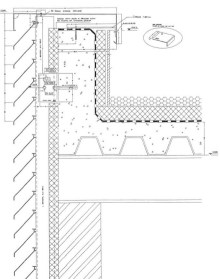

Section through parapet over boiler room.

designed in such a way that the facade still remains completely flat. This flush facade surface was part of the minimalist approach of the architects. The construction rests on a lattice of Curtal circular aluminium tubes which act as an internal loadbearing structure provided with a double seal (silicone outside and EPDM inside).

Materials: The supporting lattice for the structural glazing curtain wall was realized with the aid of Siltal standard sections. The exposed internal and external components were anodized and given a satin finish with the help of a chemical process. The non-exposed parts were fabricated from untreated aluminium. The infill panels are clamped to the supporting lattice using aluminium scaffold fixings, also untreated. The vertical members of the curtain wall are suspended from the concrete floors of the building. The opening windows have an outer stop achieved with Siltal standard sections. Opening of the windows is controlled by a reversed type CE2G Bercy espagnolette which is fitted to the lower horizontal member of the frame.

The opaque 27 mm sandwich panels consist of:
–   an outer aluminium sheet with a thickness of 20 x 0.1 mm, anodized (coating thickness 20 μm) with a chemical satin surface finish without prior mechanical treatment of the surface,
–   polyurethane thermal insulation,
–   an untreated aluminium sheet with a thickness of 20 x 0.1 mm.

The panels are 1344 mm high and the width varies depending on the respective module. The junction between the spandrel panel and the horizontal fire stop (60 min. fire resistance) is achieved with a special aluminium section. The fire stop is placed in front of the edge of the concrete floor slab and consists of two Promatect boards each 25 mm thick and a filling of mineral wool. Another aluminium section joins the curtain wall with the vertical fire stop consisting of 12 mm thick Promatect boards. These boards are attached to a separate metal framework independent of the curtain wall at a height of 680 mm above the concrete floor slab.

Address: 23, avenue Arnaud Fraiteur, Brussels, Belgium
Architects: Samyn & Partners, Brussels
P. Samyn, M. Ruelle, Q. Steyaert, J. Ceyssens, A. Agustsdottir, G. André, T. Andersen, M. Bergmans, A. Brodsky, Y. Buyle, D. Culot, K. Delafontaine, J.P. Dequenne, B. Dewancker, I. Iglesias Martin Benito, F. Lermusiaux, N. Milo, M. Van Raemdonck, O. Verhaeghe, C. Zurek, in collaboration with A+U (J. Baudon)
Consulting engineers: Setesco, G. Clantin, J. Schiffmann, P. Samyn (structure);
Marco et Roba (services)
Client: Louis de Waele SA, real estate developers
Construction period: 1992-98
Aluminium components: Sital system, Curtal sections
Fabricator: Portal Belgium

The sunshades, the structure, the walls
and the roof are detached from each other,
and the white aluminium panels symbolize
the technological vocation of the college.

45° splayed end adjacent to the road.

HIGHER TECHNICAL FEDERAL SCHOOL

Ernst Giselbrecht

Design: The underlying concept of the Kaindorf Higher
Technical Federal School for IT, organization and automation is that
of a village. Various sections with classrooms stretch out like wings
to both sides of the 170 m long, two-storey, central block. The
sports hall with its northlight roof provides a counterpoint to the
horizontal orientation of the main building and its lateral wings. The
branching layout of the complex permits the inclusion of external
biotopes, which serve as the extension to a series of terraces to
create areas that can also be used for leisure and relaxation. The
very explicit presence of the structure and the architectural details
is a symbol for the technological objectives of the college. This
approach akin to utilitarian architecture, particularly evident in the
structure and the sunshades, is the «signature» for the appearance
of this complex.

Construction: All the blocks of the complex are based on
the same constructional concept. Two storeys with utility areas
(classrooms etc.) are linked by a central corridor which runs
through the whole building, with the side walls omitted at some
points (library etc.) so that a clear and open atmosphere is
generated. Four rows of circular reinforced concrete columns
support the upper floor and divide the main building and the lateral
wings into two parts with teaching or administration rooms
separated by corridors. The end of the long main building and the
block placed at 45° to the road define the relationship between the
buildings and their mature surroundings, and prepare us for the
main entrance. Trusses support the roof covering. The facade
cladding does not extend as far as the roof but instead stops below

Site layout.

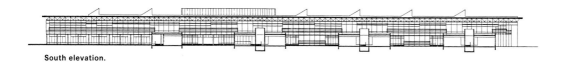

South elevation.

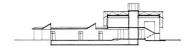

Section.

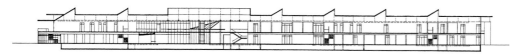

Longitudinal section.

The play of light and shade on the facade.

Axonometric view of facade.

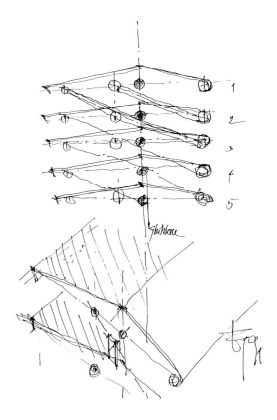

Design study for movable sunshades.

The movable sunshades of perforated aluminium.

Facade detail.

The movable louvres and lattice girder supporting
the roof.

a lattice girder which carries the roof structure and constitutes an architectural feature – like a high-level window running along beneath the roof.

Materials: The facades are clad in white aluminium panels. The sunshades make use of a new system having movable perforated aluminium panels. These are suspended from the roof and, as a demonstrative technological element, form part of the system of superimposed layers which separate the interior from the exterior. The line of the windows is protected by rotating and sliding louvres whose movement imitates the brake flaps of an aeroplane. These perforated aluminium louvres, operated by means of scissor hinges, control the amount of heat and light entering the interior. In this system every individual part can be separately controlled; however, once a day all sunshades are synchronized in order to give the complete complex a harmonious overall impression again. The supporting construction for the glazed curtain wall and the window frames are also made from aluminium sections.

Address: Kaindorf, Austria
Architect: Ernst Giselbrecht with
Werner Kircher, Kurt Falle, Wolfgang Ellmaier, Zsolt Gunther, Kuno Kelih, Andreas Moser, Gerhard Springer, Klaus Faber (project team)
Client: Kaindorf Local Authority
Consulting engineers: Heidinger, Aigner, Pölzl (structure);
Essler Consultants (electrical services); Ing. Starchel Consultants (HVAC)
Construction period: 1988-94
Aluminium components: cladding of white aluminium panels,
sunshades of perforated aluminium
Fabricators: Schüco sections (glazed curtain wall and window frames), Ludwig Brandstaetter, Frohnleiten, Austria (panels and aluminium elements), Treiber, Graz, Austria (development of sunshade system)

The northlight roof provides ample daylight in the sports hall.

The workshops on the northern part of the site.

View along the facade.

Fixed louvres in front of loadbearing walls, movable ones in front of window openings.

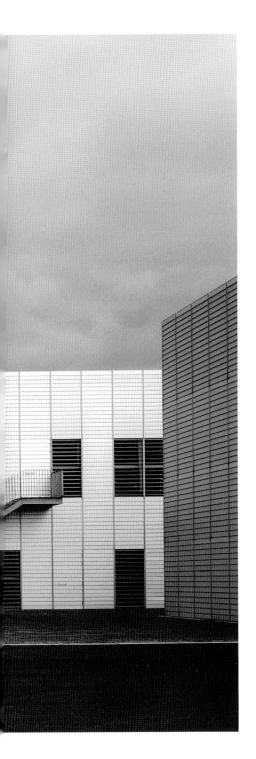

BOOK TECHNOLOGY CENTRE

Dominique Perrault

Design: The «Centre Technique Du Livre» in Bussy-Saint-Georges was built at the same time as the Bibliothèque de France François Mitterrand. This centre accommodates bookbinding workshops and part of the library's bookstack. This is where the obligatory copies of works not intended for general distribution are stored together with those books of the Ile-de-France university libraries (dissertations and periodicals) less frequently asked for. Apart from the storage rooms, this complex includes facilities for transferring works to microfilm, deacidification and conservation of the papers and digital compilation, a laboratory and a training centre for conservation methods. The centre is situated on the A4 motorway adjacent to Line A of the regional express railway link which cuts the journey time from Marne-la-Vallée to the centre of Paris to less than 30 minutes. It was built during the first phase of a development programme for the Bussy-sud area, along the western boundary of this area, thus providing options for future extensions to the north, south and east. A glass-roofed passage runs through the building along an east-west axis, past the workshops and storage rooms. The workshops, offices, conference and training facilities are accommodated in six two-storey buildings arranged perpendicular to the road on the northern side. The five-storey storage buildings are situated on the southern part of the site.

Construction: Reinforced concrete walls, 250 mm thick, on a 7.2 m grid, form the loadbearing structure.

Materials: Aluminium louvres have been used for the cladding to the 9 m high workshop facades and the 15 m high facades to the

View through the window of a training room.

Training room with loadbearing wall of reinforced concrete and aluminium frames in the background.

Internal walkway with metal frame.

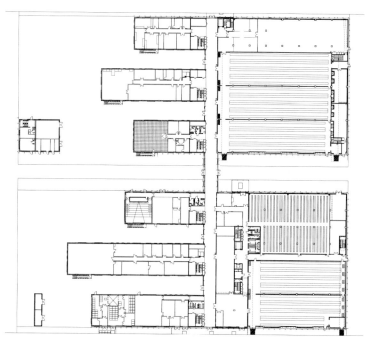

Plan of ground floor.

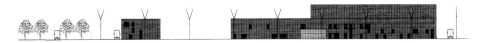

East elevation.

Elevation with section through internal passage linking the storage facilities with the buildings housing workshops and training rooms.

The strict geometry of the aluminium louvres fits in well with the transparency of the Batyline canopy over the unloading bay.

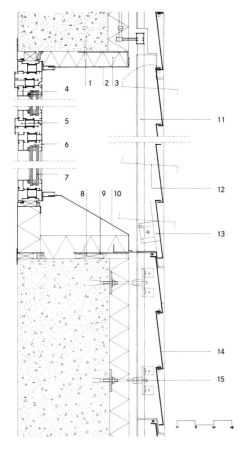

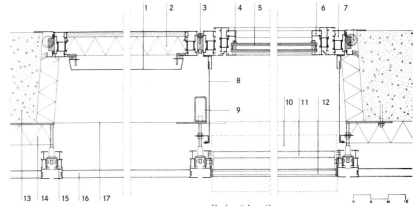

Section through loadbearing external wall.
1. Concrete
2. Head and jamb of light metal alloy
3. Thermal insulation
4. Joint
5. Aluminium frame to opening light
6. Aluminium frame to fixed light
7. Glazing
8. Timer batten
9. Steel sheet
10. Continuous sloping sill
11. Movable frame
12. Space for movable aluminium section
13. Movable aluminium section
14. Fixed aluminium cladding
15. Fixing for movable aluminium frame

Horizontal section.
1. Protective steel cover
2. Composite panel of light metal alloy
3. Steel section
4. Joint
5. Glazing
6. Aluminium frame to opening light
7. Aluminium frame
8. Aluminium sheet cladding
9. Steel section, 70 x 35 mm
10. Space for opening section
11. Connecting tube
12. Movable section
13. Concrete
14. Thermal insulation
15. Aluminium section
16. Fixed composite panel of light metal alloy
17. Outside edge of concrete

storage buildings. The louvres in front of the opaque sections of the facades are fixed and those in front of window openings movable by way of electric servomotors. The horizontal louvres are all 1120 mm long x 150 mm wide and just 1 mm thick. The aluminium cladding is fixed to the reinforced concrete walls by way of intermediate aluminium frames. The window frames are also made from aluminium.

Address: Parc d'activités Gustave Eiffel, Bussy-Saint-Georges, France
Architects: Dominique Perrault;
Maxime Gaspérini (authorized signatory), Jérôme Besse (assistant architect)
Client: Bibliothèque Nationale de France, Ministry for Higher Education and Research
Auditors: Pieffet-Corbin
Consulting engineers: Daniel Allaire (engineer); Séchaud et Boussuyt (structure);
TPS (HGM); Technip Seri Construction (fluids and piped services); Syseca (security);
Guy Huguet S.A. (air-conditioning and central control of services)
Construction period: 1993-95
Aluminium components: panels designed by the architects

The cladding during erection.

View of north facade showing composite aluminium panels to projecting bays.

The east facade, with long, white-painted aluminium panels over
the opaque sections of the curtain wall to the office facades.

RENAULT PROTOTYPE DEVELOPMENT CENTRE – LE PROTO

Jean-Paul Hamonic

Design: The Centre de Réalisation des Prototypes (CRP)
represents one essential component in Renault's technology centre
at Guyancourt. This is, so to speak, the veritable heartbeat of the
creative side of Renault – the building where research and studies
for vehicle developments are brought together, prototypes
developed and manufacturing processes validated. «Le Proto», as
the building is called by Renault, consists of a 42 000 m² production
hall adjoining three modules which accommodate 5000 m² of
ancillary services. The complex comprises:
– The production area with all the plant necessary for producing
prototypes (presses, moulds, shaping, welding, painting, plastic
technology, measurements, etc.);
– assembly lines for various prototypes;
– areas in which the manufacturing processes are validated and
developed up to series production level on the main assembly
lines. The centre has a workforce of 630 producing 1–2 prototypes
per day.

Construction: The building envelope includes dominant
metal modules punctuated at regular intervals by the windows.
These windows allow plenty of daylight into the production hall,
which gives this a friendly character and good working conditions.
The materials express the various functions of the complex: at the
bottom polished concrete slabs with white marble aggregate,
facades with horizontal metal ribs or joints, and the vertical metal
ribs to sides of the monitor-like roof.
The requirements of the manufacturing process were critical for the
design of the structural steelwork (columns and trusses). Large,

Detail sections north facade.

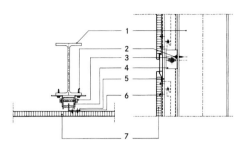

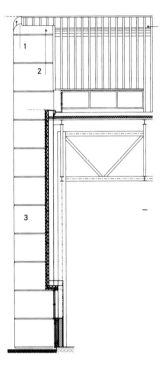

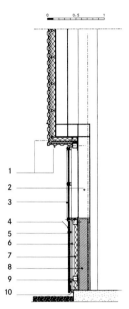

1 Curved aluminium cladding
2 Toroid-shaped aluminium cladding
3 Plain aluminium cladding with internal honeycomb structure

1 Twin-leaf facade: horizontal ribbed facade element on vertical spacers + thermal insulation + backing sheet with sound and thermal insulation
2 Secondary supporting construction for fixing the backing sheet
3 Row of windows
4 Facade element of polished concrete
5 Fixings
6 Stainless steel post
7 Thermal insulation
8 Wall of concrete blocks, plastered both sides
9 Horizontal rail
10 Continuous apron

Vertical section through plain panel.
1 Secondary supporting construction
2 Self-drilling screw (stainless steel)
3 Stainless steel bolt
4 Galvanized steel channel section
5 Aluminium angle, 30 x 10 mm
6 Pop rivet
7 formaplan:
– untreated aluminium, internal 20 x 0.1 mm
– aluminium honeycomb structure, 18 mm
– painted aluminium sheet, external 20 x 0.1 mm

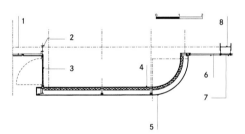

Horizontal section through plain panel.
1 Insulated metal panel
2 Secondary supporting construction
3 Glass door
4 Twin-leaf facade: vertical ribbed facade panel on backing sheet with thermal insulation
5 Plain aluminium cladding on honeycomb structure
6 Row of windows
7 Thermal insulation
8 Primary supporting construction

unobstructed areas were called for and the roof trusses had to be designed to carry the loads of many of the components being manufactured as well as plant and machinery necessary for manufacturing and controlling those components. This led to the erection of a series of frames with spans of 22.95 and 30 m on a 10.8 m grid, with generous headroom of 7, 10 and 13 m.

Materials: The aims and requirements which were defined by the architects Valode and Pistre in their specification for the Renault building in Guyancourt have been implemented as a total concept in this centre. This is particularly evident from the arrangement of the metal cladding to the external facades. The individual facades have very different appearances. The dominating north facade is given an animated character thanks to a succession of sections clad with metal sheeting – metaphorical reminders of the bodywork processes in automotive engineering. The south facade allows for extension. At the west facade deliveries of materials take place, while the ancillary services are concealed behind the east facade.

The plinth to each facade consists of polished concrete slabs (with white marble aggregate; 1200 x 1200 x 30 mm, with 80 mm mineral fibre thermal insulation) which are attached to a stainless steel framework by means of spigots. This framework is in turn attached to the main structural steelwork of the building. The double-glazed windows (Master Line products from St Gobain for security reasons) are fitted into aluminium frames (Kawneer sections) and are up to 6 m high. The continuous sections of the twin-leaf facade comprise outer steel sheets with ribs spaced at 125 mm mounted on spacers

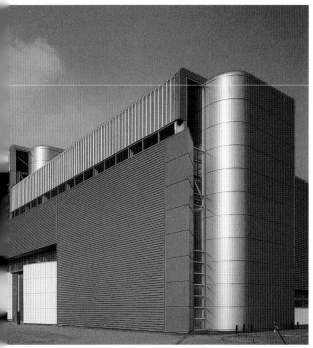
The west facade.

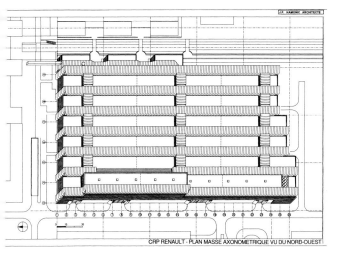
Axonometric plan, viewed from north-west.

CRP RENAULT - PLAN MASSE AXONOMETRIQUE VU DU NORD-OUEST

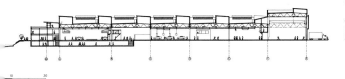
East-west section.

and fitted internally with a perforated sheet to improve sound insulation. Between these two sheets there are two layers of mineral wool laid with staggered joints. In certain areas (press etc.) a third cladding layer of 1 mm sheet was added, fixed centrally over the joints of the inner sheets (Smac Acieroid system), to achieve better sound insulation for the neighbouring rooms. The roof is covered with ribbed steel sheets similar to those used for the facade; however, the ribs to the sides of the monitor-like roof run vertically and are spaced at 300 mm. This creates a relief in both the longitudinal and transverse direction. Ingress of water is prevented by means of a slate-grey multilayer membrane supported by a backing sheet, to improve sound insulation, with 80 mm Panotoit-Quatro thermal insulation from St Gobain.

The north facade borders a principal access road which crosses the technology centre. To reinforce its effect, the lateral ends of the monitor-type roofs, which allow plenty of daylight to enter the workshops, are highlighted by projecting bays the full height of the building. These are clad with Karen panels consisting of two plain aluminium sheets (grey metallic paint RAL 9006) bonded to an aluminium honeycomb structure. These very large panels measure 1.25 m high and are 5.50 m long between their quarter-circle rounded ends (radius 1.50 m). These panels were fabricated by Axter on a timber jig under vacuum. The panels forming the transition to the roof – 4 mm aluminium sheets – were given their rounded shape while on the timber jig by using an automatic hammer. All components are attached to the thermally insulated vertical structural steelwork using concealed fixings. The east facade, with the entrances to the CRP as well as three service modules, has long, white-painted aluminium panels over the opaque sections of the curtain wall to the office facades.

Address: Technocentre Renault, Guyancourt, France
Architect: Jean-Paul Hamonic;
Patricia Gauchon (project manager), Valérie Naintre (assistant)
Client: Renault
Consulting engineers: Sofresid (construction); OPC (project management); CEP (inspection)
Bauzeit: 1995
Aluminium components: Karen aluminium panels with a 75 x 1 mm, honeycomb core with a mesh size of 19 mm to which the inner and outer sheets are bonded with the aid of a hot glue technique; outer sheets are prepainted aluminium, 20 x 0.1 mm, inner sheets untreated aluminium, 15 x 0.1 mm. Secondary supporting structure consists of untreated aluminium angle sections attached by adjustable fixings and stainless steel screwed connections.
Fabricators: Eurofaçade (Karen aluminium composite panels);
Smac-Acieroid Kawneer (aluminium frame sections); Ilfer (aluminium sections)

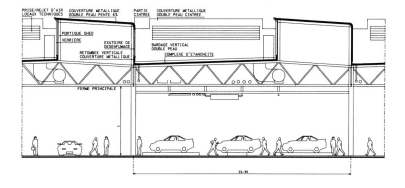
Section through one production bay.

Site layout. The thoroughfare cutting diagonally
through the centre also continues beyond
the centre in the same direction and links up with
another path on the other side of the basin.

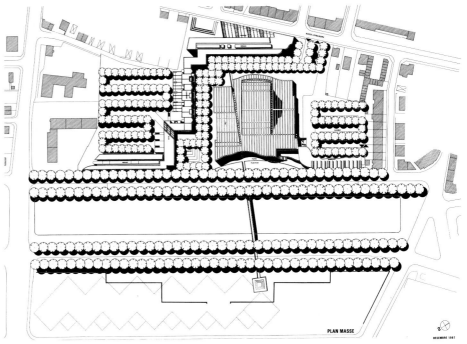

PLAN MASSE

DECEMBRE 1987

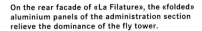

On the rear facade of «La Filature», the «folded» aluminium panels of the administration section relieve the dominance of the fly tower.

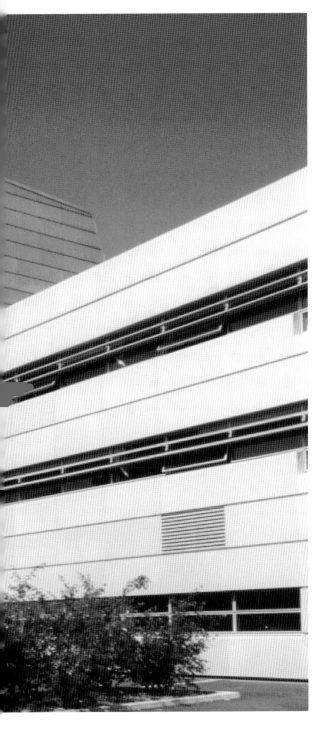

Site layout. The thoroughfare cutting diagonally through the centre also continues beyond the centre in the same direction and links up with another path on the other side of the basin.

ARTS AND CULTURAL CENTRE – LA FILATURE

Claude Vasconi

Design: Like a sphinx of the industrial age, this arts centre with its facade of aluminium and glass sits on the bank of a large basin on the site of a former spinning mill (French: «filature»), an industrial wasteland that is now being put to new use. It is the first building of a whole new district which will emerge here and will eventually include housing, shops, a sports hall and offices. This arts and cultural centre with its regional catchment area accommodates a large concert/opera hall with 1216 seats (plus those for disabled), a 350-seat dividable hall, a small hall with seating for 100, an exhibition hall, a rehearsal hall, a cinema, a library/mediatheque, a restaurant, service levels, administration areas, etc. The total area is 21 500 m^2.

The building itself was designed to be as compact as possible so that all these facilities could be accommodated in a building about 100 m long. The problem of the prominent fly tower was resolved by cladding the external walls of the building in this area right up to roof level with aluminium panels which have continuous horizontal folds reminiscent of the decorative piping on textiles. The west-east connection between the north field and the large basin cuts right through the 35 m high complex. This link runs diagonally: starting at the sports hall, it passes through the office block, becomes a glazed gallery in the arts centre and then crosses the basin on the east side. It continues over the canal by way of a footbridge, following the urban planning concept to link the two city districts situated on either side of the canal. This thoroughfare divides up the building. Therefore, the opera hall and its foyer are integrated in the urban fabric, forming a close tie between the arts centre and the city. The north-west and south-east elevations have curving facades, while

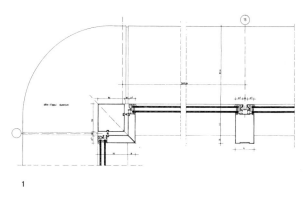

1

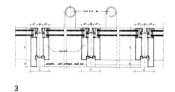

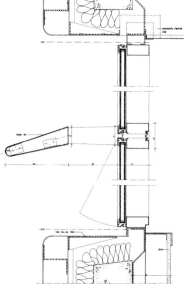

2

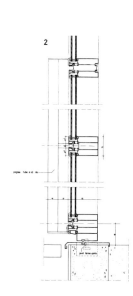

3

Details of external facade, aluminium external door and aluminium window frames.
1   Horizontal section through fixed light frame, main facade
2   Section through external door
3   Horizontal section through external door
4   Section through rear facade, sunshade

4

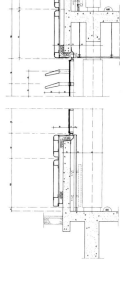

Section through rear facade.

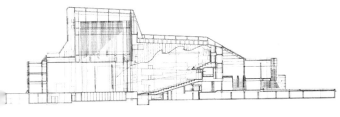

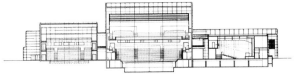

Sections through the large hall. As the hall is only 26 m deep, the 800 seats in the stalls and the 400 seats in the circle are comparatively close to the stage.

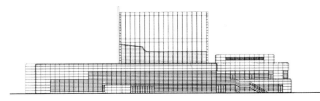

The entrance and park facades are both clad with natural-colour anodized aluminium panels.

the two side facades are straight. The form of the rhythmic, undulating facade either side of the main entrance and overlooking the forecourt takes up the idea of the small waves which the wind whips up on the surface of the water of the basin in front of the building. This generates an impression of movement which invites the observer to enter the building. The entrance foyer extends over three storeys; from here you can reach all the different sections of the arts centre. Wide stairs lead to an upper foyer where glazed concrete surfaces are a particular feature. This lies opposite the large concert hall which, like the external facades, is clad with aluminium panels. This large hall encompasses a volume of 9300 m³.

Construction: «La Filature» arts centre has a loadbearing structure of reinforced concrete and is clad completely with natural-colour anodized aluminium panels. This cladding was produced using an elaborate process and required the manufacture of a large number of different and, in some cases, curved and dished sheets (notably those for the corners).

Materials: The aluminium panels of the facade are made from 3 mm aluminium sheet. The thermal insulation attached to the reinforced concrete walls is protected by the 100 mm deep panels with vertical joints every 1 m. The aluminium sunshades, the window and door frames, with a cross-section of 75 x 115 mm and incorporating a thermal break, and various other aluminium components consummate the uniform overall appearance determined by the materials aluminium and glass. These materials are also very much in the foreground in the foyers.

Address: 20, Allée Nathan Katz, Mulhouse, France
Architects: Claude Vasconi; Jean Condorcet, Blandine Roche, Guy Turin, Bénédicte Ollier (project assistants); Y. Amstoutz, J.-P. Bobacher (local project architects)
Client: Mulhouse Municipal Authority
Consulting engineers: GIA, Strasbourg/Mulhouse; BSM, Strasbourg (building acoustics); M. Rioualec, Sceaux (stage facilities); Cano-François, Paris (3D installations)
Construction period: 1988-93
Aluminium components: prefabricated natural-colour anodized, satin-finish aluminium panels trimmed on site, consisting of 3 mm and 1.5 mm (for the non-accessible internal surfaces) aluminium sheet from Almet (Pechiney) and Alcan; aluminium alloy Al-Mg 5005 (NFA 02.104) – Rhenalu-Pechiney
Fabricators: Rinaldi (facade construction and fabrication); Pechiney, Alcan

The main entrance viewed from the canal.

The Design Center on the Mercedes-Benz site in
Sindelfingen is reminiscent of a fan.

MERCEDES-BENZ DESIGN CENTER

Renzo Piano Building Workshop

Design: A design centre has security regulations almost as strict as those of a military research establishment. In the realm of new developments in the automotive industry, industrial espionage is steadily on the increase. Therefore, a design centre must not only guard against the unwanted intrusions of the public but also those of the other departments within the same company! So the Mercedes-Benz Design Center represents, on the one hand, an extension to the huge company site in Sindelfingen, but on the other, it must be isolated from other areas. However, this separation must in no way hamper the indispensable internal communication vital for the circulation of ideas. The building resembles an open fan, with the individual «folds» each housing a different function: conception, design, model development, prototypes, etc. There are seven «folds», increasing in length from south to north, which radiate from a common centre at an angle of 9° to each other. At the eastern end of the three shortest sections there is a building which serves for displaying the models, giving the buildings with their northlight roofs another face. This section aimed at the public is separated from the main building but nevertheless linked to it via the neighbouring block housing general service facilities. The geometry of the roof of this showroom is identical to that of the (toroidal) northlight roofs of the main building – only that here the roof is transparent. On the underside of the roof there are huge opalescent sunshades with a lens-shaped cross-section which can be used to regulate the amount of incoming daylight. There is a communal garden on the north-west side of the complex.

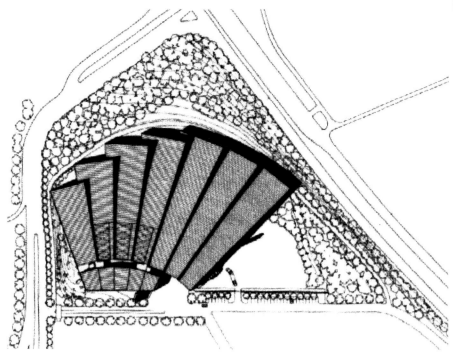

Site layout.

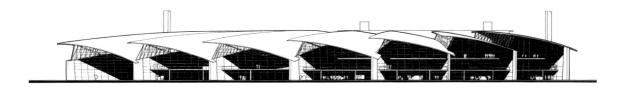

North-west elevation, facing the garden.

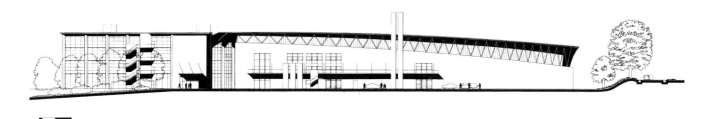

North elevation.

The curved northlight roofs allow plenty of daylight into the building.

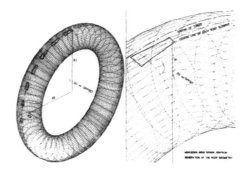

The roof design is based on the geometry of a toroid.

The north side is clad with aluminium panels bonded to a polyethylene core.

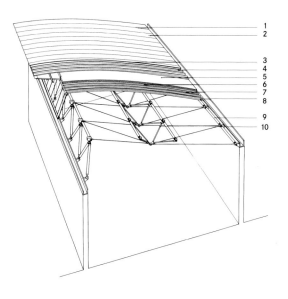

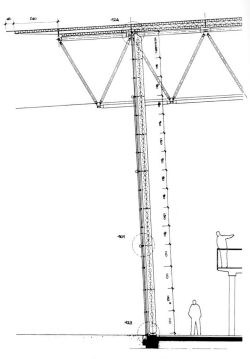

Section through west facade.

Isometric view of roof system.
1   Fixing rail for roof panels
2   Roof covering, 4 mm Alucobond
3   EPDM foil
4   Upper layer of 106 mm trapezoidal
    profile sheeting
5   180 mm thermal insulation
6   1 mm steel sheet vapour barrier
7   Sound insulation and ribs
8   Lower layer of 106 mm trapezoidal profile
    sheeting, perforated
9   Steel supporting construction
10 Centre struts of supporting construction

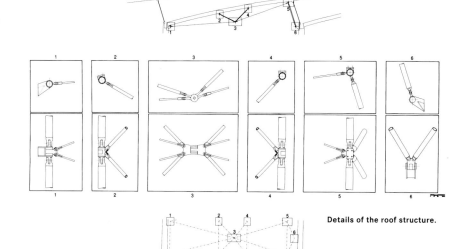

Details of the roof structure.

**Tension rods maintain the curve of
the roof covering.**

Construction: The curved roof surfaces of the individual sections are arranged like northlight roofs, which allow daylight to enter through their taller sides. The areas of glazing in the northlight roofs run in a north-west to north-east direction so that the incoming light does not cause any glare. Instead of the conventional windows at the level of the working area, such an arrangement ensures adequate daylight inside the building but also satisfies security requirements. The curved northlight roofs have been given a generous overlap with the radiating walls, particularly on the taller sides. The glazed upper sections of these walls slope towards the inside of the respective section of the building. The opening between the walls and the roofs, and hence the area of glazing, widens towards the north-west end of the building and so allows more light to enter. The long spans of the roof structure become a complicated system of columns, connecting members and tension rods which transfer the forces in the curved roof down to the foundations.

Materials: The loadbearing walls are made from in-situ concrete and are clad with special aluminium panels having a polyethylene core. This core ensures that the panels remain completely flat. The roof covering, whose form is based on segments of a three-dimensional toroidal element, consists of several metal layers. Starting from the bottom, the supporting construction carries a sandwich panel, steel trapezoidal profile sheeting with a rib depth of 106 mm is placed directly on this and covered with a 1 mm plain steel sheet acting as the vapour barrier, onto which the 180 mm thermal insulation is laid, which is then covered by another layer of steel trapezoidal profile sheeting, again with a rib depth of 106 mm. An EPDM foil separates the 4 mm Alucobond roof finish from the steel sheet underneath. Alucobond is an aluminium composite material consisting of two layers of 0.5 mm Peraluman-100 foil (AW-5005/AlMg1) enclosing a thermoplastic synthetic layer (low-density polyethylene).

The walls to the radiating fan shape are also clad with aluminium sheeting.

Address: Sindelfingen, Stuttgart, Germany
Architects: Renzo Piano Building Workshop
Client: Mercedes-Benz AG
Consultants: Ove Arup & Partners, IFB Dr. Braschel & Partner GmbH; Ove Arup & Partners, FWT Project and site supervision Mercedes-Benz AG; Müller BBM; F. Santolini
Construction period: 1993-98
Aluminium components: Alucobond
Fabricator: Algroup/Alusuisse

The amount of incoming daylight can be regulated by means of the opalescent sunshades with their lens-shaped cross-section.

The east facade.

TELEVISA BUILDING

TEN Arquitectos

Design: This multipurpose building belonging to the major television broadcaster Televisa occupies a trapezoidal plot among the urban «chaos» of downtown Mexico City. The new building concludes a series of blocks which accommodate the administrative functions of the television company. The eight-storey office block on the eastern side of the plot and the transmission mast form undeniable urban boundaries. The Televisa Building replaces a group of small buildings which until 1995 had accommodated the same functions: offices, conference rooms, meeting rooms, a staff canteen and parking. In this urban landscape it serves as an emblem for the presence of the television station. The building comprises two distinct superimposed units which communicate in different ways with the road on one side and the city on the other on two different scales. With its black monolithic facade, the parking zone correlates with the road as part of the urban space. The elliptical aluminium shell echoes the morphological tumult of this very densely developed part of the city and accommodates common facilities such as 600-seat canteen, cafeteria, kitchen, bar, meeting rooms, conference rooms, etc. The transparent glass facade of the service level links the parking zone with the shell above. The reference to a vernacular industrial architecture permits the interjection of modernism without ostentation.

Construction: The earthquake-resistant reinforced concrete walls as well as the reinforced concrete floors supported by steel lattice girders constitute the basic structure of the building. The tapering elliptical aluminium shell makes use of structural members with various cross-sections which constitute the supporting,

Exterior view. The aluminium shell rests on a ground floor storey containing parking and offices.

Exterior view in the evening light. The aluminium
shell poses a contrast to the vertical orientation of
the transmitter mast.

Interior view.

Interior view.

parallel «side walls». The metal purlins, which carry the actual roof covering, are placed on these «sides» corresponding to the tapering form. The roof construction, from inside to outside, consists of a three-part pinewood layer (19 mm thick), an Omega aluminium profile, an impermeable bituminous vapour barrier and Alucobond sheeting with butyl rubber joints as the outermost layer.

Materials: The curved roof is provided with a covering of Alucobond sheeting of various dimensions. The external walls of the building below are clad with black concrete panels. Alucobond sheeting is also used for the cladding to the kitchen block. The lift shaft is constructed from fair-face concrete, the entrance area is clad with prepatinated zinc composite panels. The circulation zones in the upturned cone have a ceramic tile finish. Glass walls enclose the access ramp.

Address: 32, avenida Chapultepec, Mexico City, Mexico
Architects: TEN Arquitectos – Enrique Norten, Bernardo Gomez-Pimienta (project architects); Blanca Castañeda, Raul Acevedo, Jesus Alfredo Dominguez, Gustavo Espitia, Héctor L. Gámiz, Rebeca Golden, Margarita Goyzueta, Javier Presas, Roberto Sheinberg, Maria Carmen Zeballos (project team)
Client: Televisa SA de C.V.
Consulting engineers: Guy Nordenson, Ove Arup & Partners, New York; Colinas de Buen, Mexico (structure); AMS Derby, Inc. - Robert Harbinson (roof)
Construction period: 1993-95
Aluminium components: Alucobond panels, window frames of natural-colour anodized aluminium
Fabricator: Algroup/Alusuisse

The staff canteen is enclosed by the aluminium shell.

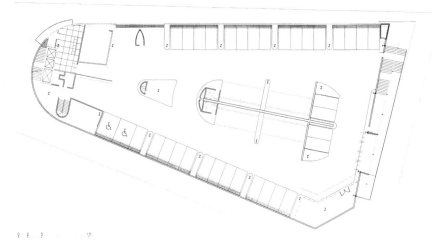

Plan of ground floor showing
access and parking

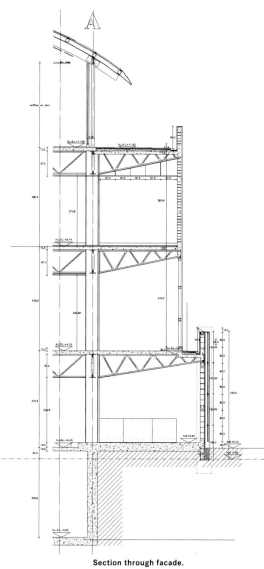

Section through facade.

View of complex.

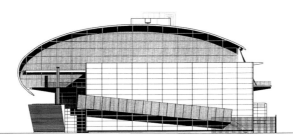

South elevation.

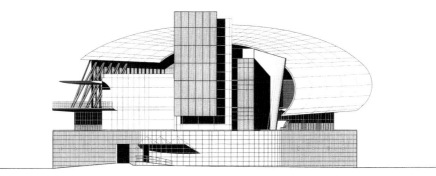

North elevation showing aluminium shell.

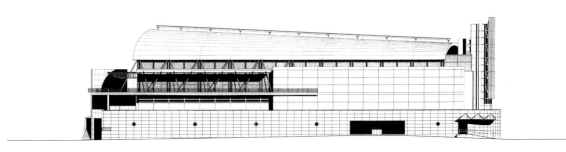

East elevation.

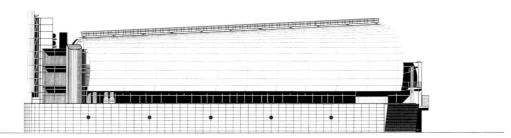

West elevation showing aluminium shell.

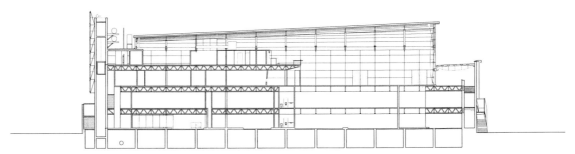

Longitudinal section.

View of the centre from the canal.

View of the centre from the park.

View of the centre from the park.

REIMS CONVENTION CENTRE

Claude Vasconi

Design: Situated at the intersection of various traffic routes (Paris-Strasbourg motorway, Aisne Canal, River Vesle, etc.), this convention centre represents a sort of gateway to the city of Reims. The site of a former quayside warehouse complex, this position adjacent to the Aisne Canal was the optimum location for this long, serene edifice with its aluminium cladding. The convention centre is elevated above the ground and borders the «Patte d'Oie» Park, a landscaped area with a good stock of mature trees. However, the view towards the canal, towards the south, is not obstructed. The actual building itself is placed 5 m above the ground on «stilts» and is only anchored to the ground at a few places. This elevated arrangement results in several advantages: Boulevard Maurice Noirot can pass beneath between two rows of stilts thus making it possible to erect the congress centre directly on the former quayside. Keeping the ground floor open enables the exhibition area to be doubled if necessary. And finally, the building gains an unusual feature which further emphasizes its symbolic significance. The entrance foyer is located behind the fully glazed north facade facing the park. The stairs and escalators take visitors directly to the large exhibition hall, the foyers of the two congress halls as well as the large restaurants (with seating for 1000) «perched» among the treetops of the park. The exhibition hall, the Clovis Hall (capacity 350 persons) and the «Royal» Hall (capacity 720 persons) determine the rising ceilings of the interior, which reach a total height of 27 m, i.e. corresponding to the height of the large hall. The Clovis and Royal halls are quasi «suspended» over the foyer. The complex is laid out in such a way that the view of the cathedral from the motorway is not obstructed.

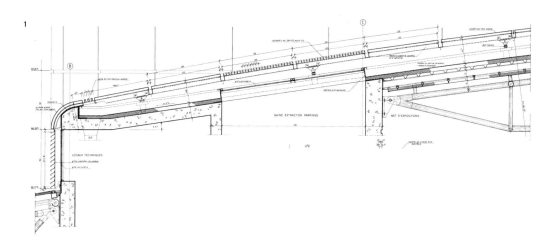

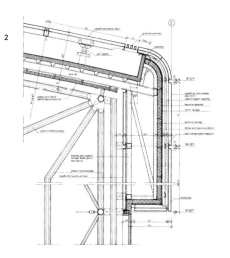

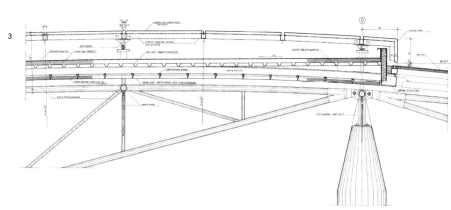

Detail of covering and cladding to exhibition hall.
1   Section through roof construction to exhibition hall and plant rooms
2   Section through north facade to exhibition hall
3   Section through roof, exhibition hall glazing

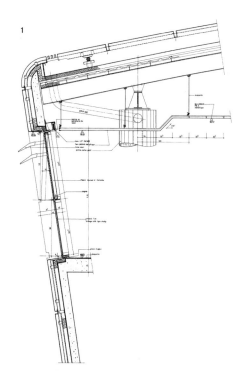

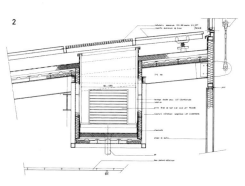

Details of «suspended» halls.
1   Full height glazing
2   Exhaust air ducting

Interior view of congress hall.

Site layout.

Longitudinal section through canal side.

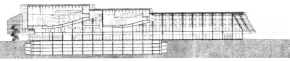
Longitudinal section through park side.

Park elevation.

Canal elevation.

Bar, cloakrooms and the kitchen serving the restaurants are all in the bottom storey. The spacious flanking gallery passes through the part of the building next to the canal. This southern wing houses meeting rooms separated from each other by way of lightwells. The administration section, which is located below the meeting rooms, borders the large exhibition hall, which is connected to the forecourt at ground level via a shallow ramp. This forecourt is given a certain transparency thanks to its partly open, partly covered design, and forms the roof to a car park for 250 vehicles. The foyers are provided with wide stairs whose geometry and special arrangement lend them a very expressive quality.

Construction: The loadbearing structure comprises columns, floor slabs and reinforced concrete elements. The «suspended» structures of the various halls make use of reinforced concrete walls. Concealed structural steelwork (IPE sections etc.) carries the various cladding elements and finishes of the building. The exhibition hall has delicate steel frames resting on very slender columns whose tops resemble «the point of a pencil». HEA 120 sections lie above on this framework, supported on intermediate «vertical journals». Painted (aluminium-colour), perforated steel plates are suspended from the HEA sections; these have a layer of felt for sound insulation purposes. These plates in turn carry trays of steel trapezoidal profile sheeting in which thermal insulation type Panotoit (100 mm) and a vapour barrier (two layers) are placed. Adjustable elements are arranged on «spigots» on the primary structure and these support a square grid of galvanized steel channel sections to which the aluminium cladding panels are fixed. This creates a cavity for intercepting rainwater by means of the aluminium drainage grids running along the edges of the building, and also for ventilating the underside of the aluminium panels.

Materials: The «Janus-like» character of the convention centre – closed off on the motorway side, open on the opposite (city) side – determined the choice of materials. A glazed curtain wall opens up the building on the park side, while an aluminium «carapace» closes off the motorway elevation. The facade cladding and the roof covering are made from aluminium panels using 3 mm thick aluminium sheeting which is turned up 50 mm along each edge. These panels have various dimensions as well as various geometric shapes (e.g. 1250 x 2350 x 50 mm).

Address: Parc de la Patte d'Oie, Reims, France
Architect: Claude Vasconi; Étienne Le Comte, Stéphanie Navecth, Bénédicte Ollier, Piotr Zaborski, Guido Loeckx, Hervé Basset, Jérôme Besse, Henrike Böhme, Gérard Cladière, Jean Condorcet, Emmanuelle Dambrune, Katja Gäbel, Renaud Gavach-Pepin, Alain Mazet, Christophe Pudjak, Blandine Roche, Joachim Ruoff, Cynthia Sours, Laurence Stern, Jérôme van Overbeke (project team)
Client: Reims Municipal Authority
Consulting engineers: Sudéquip (structure); XU Acoustique (acoustics); Cabinet Labeyrie (information and communication systems)
Construction period: 1990-94
Aluminium components: aluminium panels, painted, fabricated in the works and adapted on site by Durand, made from 3 mm thick aluminium sheeting supplied by Almet (Pechiney) and Alcan; light grey colour (Protime paint) by way of anodizing or baking
Fabricator: Durand structure (facade); Pechiney, Alcan

Interior view of the old workshop today.

One workshop as it was used in former times.

The old workshops at Borsig Tower.

104

REDEVELOPMENT OF BORSIG WORKS

Claude Vasconi

Design: The Borsig Works at Tegel-Reinickendorf in former West Berlin were erected in 1898 on a site covering about 60 hectares, directly adjacent to the River Havel. During the 20th century most of Germany's locomotives were built here. Following various industrial «mutations», the site was bought by the Herlitz company which, in agreement with the Berlin Senate in 1993, decided to develop a new urban concept for the entire north-east corner covering 20 hectares. The 65 m high Borsig Tower, built in 1924, has become the physical emblem of the site. This and Borsig Gate, with its turrets and arcade forming an ornamental entrance portal to Berliner Strasse, are undoubtedly among the more notable cultural monuments of this city. A genuine piece of the city is to be built on this industrial wasteland in order to link north and south Tegel. Vast commercial complexes, cinemas, leisure facilities, offices, hotels, housing, research centres and new technological establishments will emerge here on an area of 300 000 m². To reunite the River Havel with the city, an east-west axis – an urban avenue – will be created as part of the urban development project, running from Borsig Gate on Berliner Strasse, past the Borsig Tower and on to the river in the west. Part of the architectural project already realized is the workshops refurbishment at Borsig Tower. The 200 m long foundry halls have been converted, although care has been taken to avoid giving the buildings a nostalgic flavour. The concept integrates certain buildings classed as historic monuments in a new project which stretches from Berliner Strasse in the east to the large multistorey car park (capacity 1200 vehicles) in the west. In order to preserve the halls as historical documents and «recycle» them for contemporary purposes, the historically highly interesting

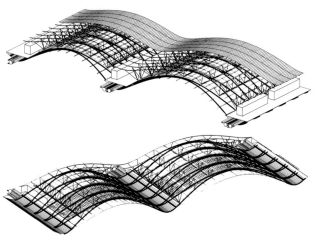

Axonometric views of the roof construction.
The glass roof is positioned below perforated panels which act as sunshades and hide the air-conditioning units.

Office block, workshops.

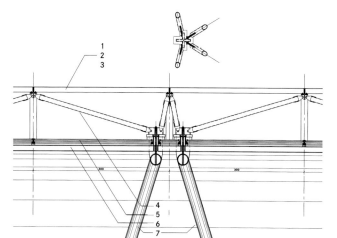

Section through roof construction.
1 Metal T-section (1/2 IPE 270)
2 Perforated aluminium sheet
3 Bird guard
4 Strut, 101.6 x 6.3 mm
5 Glazing
6 Purlin, 120 x 80 x 6.3 mm
7 Arched rib, 244.5 x 16 mm

Interior view of hall, span 43 m.

gables (3 + 2) on Werkstrasse were preserved. The concrete supporting structures, which enabled large unobstructed areas for working on the locomotives, were reappropriated for use as a commercial centre and form a new hall whose curtain wall front gable links the old, converted workshops. Large, undulating roof constructions with a skin of aluminium and glass cover the six halls of the ensemble. These roofs link the individual buildings of the project and ensure the necessary shading for the floors below. The six parallel buildings (five former workshops and one newly erected gallery) form the heart of a shopping centre – a perfect adaptation for the complex activities of such usage. This shopping centre, the cinemas complex and the areas for leisure activities extend over three storeys of the six buildings covered by the «wave» of the roof. An additional basement provides access for deliveries and supplies to the large complex. One of the old buildings became the principal pedestrian precinct for the whole project. This mall in the fourth hall (which originally contained a casting pit) is lined with trees. It connects the shopping centre at north Tegel with Borsig Tower and with Borsig Gate in the south. A number of restaurants situated in the centre of the complex constitute the east-west link from the new five-storey building on Berliner Strasse, which looks as though it is clad with oversize «razor blades» (and whose triangular layout «appeals» to pedestrians to enter the mall), to the nine-storey car park in the west. The centre also contains an area dedicated to artistic and cultural events.

Construction: Erected on the existing bays of the old halls, the new construction has a rectangular grid measuring 6 m north-

View of the aluminium roofs and undulating glazing sections.

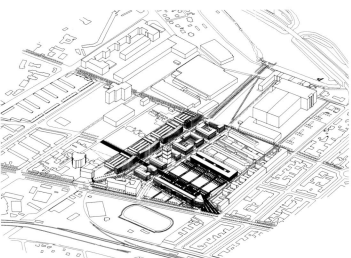
Axonometric view of the whole site.

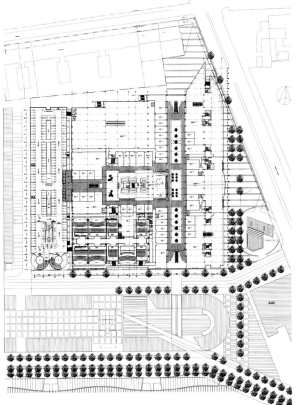
Plan of level 1.

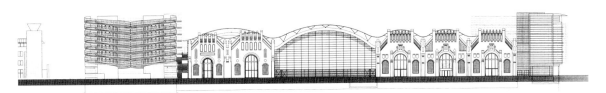
South elevation. From left to right: multistorey car park, two former workshops, new hall, three former workshops, office block.

West-east section.

Interior view of shopping mall.

south and 12-18 m east-west. The entire construction makes use of structural steelwork. The broad expanse of the roof projects a feeling of continuity punctuated by the curved supporting structures. All public spaces within the complex, the north-south mall in the fourth hall, the squares and the circulation zones are covered with glass roofs – a unifying architectural element which at the same time allows daylight to illuminate the public areas. The «wave» of the roof provides space for the building services. Therefore, large areas of the complex remain uncluttered by the numerous technical services indispensable in such a development.

Materials: The structure is painted anthracite grey. The floors to the public areas are provided with a granite covering. The shops along the mall are spaced at regular intervals thanks to the steel frame and this provides for a harmonious overall impression. Besides steel and glass, the other main material used – especially for the office block in the east – is a grey-blue painted aluminium. This was also used for the multistorey car park facades but in this case in perforated form. The perforated aluminium panels are fixed to T-sections (1/2 IPE 270) and cover the glass roofs which are supported on a framework with struts (101.6 x 6.3 mm) and purlins (120 x 80 x 6.3 mm). The supporting construction is in turn carried by arched circular hollow section ribs (244.5 x 16 mm).

The integration of the old structure.

Address: Berliner Strasse 27, Berlin-Tegel
Architect: Claude Vasconi; Dagmar Gross (assistant architect);
Guy Bez, Bruno Baudin, Jean Condorcet, Emmanuelle Dambrune, Fabienne Gallet, Mélanie Lallemand-Flucher, Guido Loeckx, Sylvie Magnin, Thierry Meunier, Bénédicte Ollier, Christophe Pudjak, Susanne Schneider, Donato Severo, Jadwiga Sowa, Cathrin Trebeljahr, Jérôme van Overbeke, Gabrielle Welisch, Claudia Wetzel (project team in Paris); Jürgen Mayer-Douarre, Matthias Hoffend, Marc Stroh, Larissa Olufs, Helga Falkenberg, Britta Heiber, Arnaud Maurel, Hervé Proby, Detlev Heintz (project team in Berlin)
Client: RSE Projektmanagement AG (formerly Herlitz Falkenhöh AG).
Consulting engineers: Prof. Polonyi + Fink GmbH, Ingenieurbüro für Bauwesen (structure); HL Technik AG and Ebert Ingenieure (services); Bau-Contor Adam and Ingenieurbüro Stefan Gräf & Partner (piling)
Construction period: 1994-99
Aluminium components: aluminium panels from Rinaldi, 2mm aluminium; perforated panels from Zambelli
Fabricator: Almet/Pechiney

Supports of the new structure.

The transport interchange deploys its wing on
the North Greenwich peninsula.

Slender struts support the roof over the 30 m wide entrance to the underground station.

GREENWICH TRANSPORT INTERCHANGE

Foster & Partners

Design: This recently erected London «portal» on the Greenwich peninsula in the vicinity of the Millennium Dome represents a fundamental component in the transport strategy of the new century. Travellers arriving from Kent and the south-west of England by bus, coach or private car can transfer here to London's public transport system. Here under one single roof we have a node in the transport network, representing an integral part of the infrastructure of the new city district developed on the Greenwich peninsula. Since the opening of the Millennium Dome, this district has been the destination for an estimated 9 million visitors; added to this are thousands of new inhabitants and workers in this part of the city. The transport interchange building was built above the North Greenwich underground station on the Jubilee Line. The hourly capacity at peak times is 76 buses, 24 underground trains (each with a capacity of 1000 passengers), 100 taxis and 100 private cars dropping off and picking up travellers. The interchange includes 11 bus stops, 16 coach parking zones and 1000 parking spaces for commuters and visitors. The transport interchange is open on and accessible from all sides, with the roof extended around the perimeter to offer travellers protection from the weather. On the «concave» side of the building, also protected by the roof reminiscent of a wing, taxis and other vehicles can drop off or pick up passengers, while the bus and coach terminals are located along the outer semicircular side of the interchange. Passengers can patiently await and see the arrival of their bus or coach from the comfort of a separate, glazed waiting room situated in the centre of this «convex side».

The lighting units suspended below the roof have two functions: one cone of light shines directly downwards, while a second strikes the aluminium panels of the roof which then reflect the light downwards to illuminate the floor indirectly.

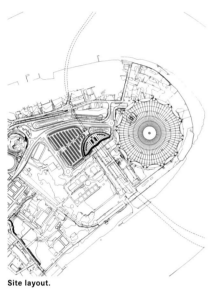

Site layout.

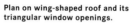

Plan on wing-shaped roof and its triangular window openings.

Plan of ground floor.

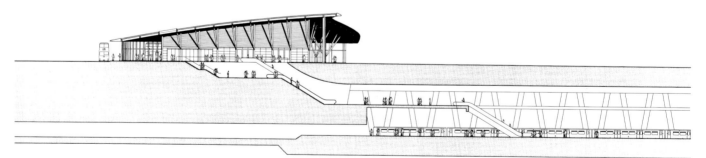

Section through entrance to underground station.

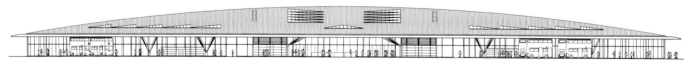

Bus terminal elevation.

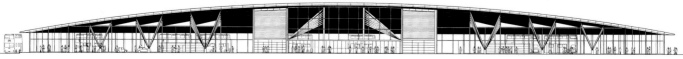

Arrivals and departures elevation.

Junction between glazed waiting room and roof.

Construction: The main element determining this concept is the shape of the roof, which is reminiscent of an outstretched wing. The roof is actually a tiny segment of the surface of a sphere with a diameter of 1 km. It spans 160 m and covers the complete interchange. The roof covering comprises reflective aluminium panels with triangular window openings which enable daylight to enter the interior. The position of the building directly above the underground station as well as the need for unrestricted circulation gave rise to this shape. The columns along the curving perimeter of the bus terminal also play the role of supports for the vertical glass facade of the waiting room (the building has a total of 2300 m² of glazing). Branching steel columns support the roof above the arrival and departure zones, and at the entrance to the underground station the roof, which here spans 30 m, is supported on slender struts. The glass facades providing protection from the weather are attached with the help of a suspended construction; open cavities permit natural ventilation. The lighting units suspended below the roof have two functions: their cone of light strikes the aluminium panels of the roof which then reflect the light downwards to illuminate the floor indirectly.

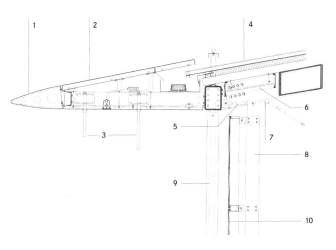
Junction between roof and glass facade to waiting room.
1 Aluminium nosing
2 Aluminium roof edge profile
3 Signage hangers
4 Aluminium standing seam roofing system
5 Movement connection (piston)
6 Extruded aluminium tube with natural anodized finish
7 Luminaire anchor point
8 Wind post
9 Mild steel external column
10 Line of glazing

Materials: The «calotte» roof, based on a sphere with a diameter of 1 km, which at its lowest point is just 5 m above the ground and at its highest 12 m, required a material which could support the necessary degree of curvature during the construction phase and which offered a multitude of shaping possibilities imposed by the curved design of the roof. The roof to the Transport Interchange consists of 6500 m² of Kalzip profiles with a natural stucco finish, 0.9 mm thick and 300 mm wide. The folded profiles are each made from one piece (max. 60 m long).
The lower steel shells of the construction comprise Kal-Dek profiles. Owing to the length of the profiles used, an innovative technology was necessary during the construction phase: mobile production units fabricated the Kalzip profiles directly on site. Portable bending machines gave the different folded profiles their final shape. The edge of the roof is made from 3 mm aluminium tubes with a polyester powder coating (RAL 9006). Anodized aluminium elements with a diameter of 50 mm were used as the ceiling panels. The glazing bars are also made from aluminium.

Address: Greenwich, London, Great Britain
Architects: Foster & Partners, London;
Sir Norman Foster with David Nelson, Robert McFarlane, David Summerfield, Russell Hales, Hannah Lehmann, Daniel Parker, Clive Powell, James Risebro
Client: London Transport, David Bailey
Consulting engineers: Anthony Hunt Associates (structure); Max Fordham & Partners (services); Claude Engle (lighting); Land Use Consultants (landscaping)
Quantity surveyors: MDA Group UK
Project management: London Underground Ltd Management Services in conjunction with Project Managers Capital Project Consultancy Ltd
Construction period: 1995-98
Aluminium components: Kalzip type 300 (65 x 300)
Fabricator: Hoogovens Aluminium International

The new northern entrance with the boulevard du
Centenaire and the Atomium behind Palais 5.

ccess to the different floors.

The timber and reinforced concrete construction.

BRUSSELS EXHIBITION CENTRE

Samyn & Partners

Design: The City of Brussels appointed the architect Joseph van Neck to design a large complex of buildings for the 1935 World Exposition. No less than 20 million visitors were expected to come to Brussels for that major event. Since then, the grounds, which also hosted the 1958 World Exposition, have been extended by numerous new buildings and in the meantime have become the leading venue in Belgium for exhibitions and other important events (auto industry fairs, leisure industry fairs, etc.). During the World Exposition of 1935 the public reached the exhibition grounds from the city centre usually by walking or by taking the tram. The entrance was marked by the colonnade and the ponds at the place de Belgique at the far end of boulevard du Centenaire. At the World Exposition in 1958, which took place on plateau du Heysel, the perspective of the entrance was not only accentuated by the new curtain wall to palais 5 (designed by Jacques Dupuis and Albert Bontridder and dismantled following the exposition) but also by establishing a central axis from Palais 5 to the Atomium (designed by André and Jean Polak). By the time of that World Exposition, the use of the car and hence the volume of traffic had increased dramatically. Brussels' roads were transformed in order to cope with the number of cars heading for the World Exposition grounds. Since then access has been more and more via the parking areas at the rear of the building; these can accommodate up to 12 000 vehicles and benefit from a direct link to the motorway. The bus terminals, most of which are also located here on chaussée Romaine, have reinforced this development. More than 70 % of all visitors (one million each year) as well as goods vehicles arrive at the «rear» of the building. Therefore, it was obvious that an infrastructure had to be created

Overall view.

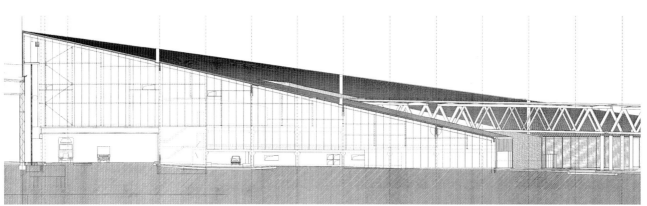

Section through entrance hall.

Interior view, central thoroughfare penetrating the
hyperbolic paraboloid.

which would make this «northern access» the real entrance. An
authentic «facade» for the Parc des Expositions (the pavilions cover
an area of 140 000 m²) was needed – like other international
exhibition centres which, after devoting themselves to the needs of
the exhibition areas, had now turned their attention to creating
large and impressive entrance zones. In designing the entrance
area, the «Princess Astrid» Pavilion, which is an important element
in the urban concept developed by Samyn & Partners, the emphasis
was on using the remaining triangular plot to the full. The new
building essentially consists of a vast hyperbolic paraboloid roof. It
is linked to the parking areas via a glass-and-timber bridge, 10 m
wide and 86 m long, which crosses chaussée Romaine. The power of
this wing-like form lies in its simple construction (cost: 446 /m²)
and the skilful use of daylight.

The tapering form of the hyperbolic paraboloid results in a narrow
and, at the same time, impressive termination to the building at the
apex of the plot. The «Princess Astrid» Pavilion, raised 6 m clear of
the ground, offers covered pedestrian access to the adjoining halls.
Stairs and escalators take visitors from the access level to the
central thoroughfare linking the exhibition halls. Delivery zones are
situated below the access level. An upper level in the building
accommodates a wide range of facilities like ticket sales, security,
information centre, reservations desk, sanitary facilities, etc. The
hyperbolic paraboloid also includes a restaurant on two levels
which is easily reached by visitors from the access level or from
outside the exhibition grounds, from the level of chaussée Romaine.
Other facilities are envisaged for the future, e.g. a business centre,
a press centre, an indoor garden and a children's playground.

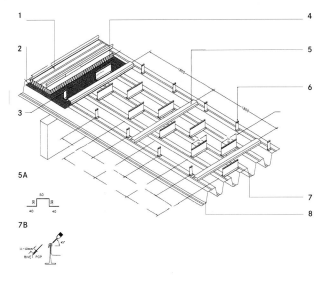

Isometric view of the roof construction.
1 Kalzip
2 Vapour barrier
3 L-100 fixing clips, with insulated cap,
   without pop rivet
4 Glass wool thermal insulation
5 Omega profile at fixing points
5A Detail of omega profile, galvanized steel, 2 mm
6 L-100 fixing clips, L = 58 mm
7 Fixing points
7B Detail of fixing point
8 Structural steel shell

Construction and materials:

The roof over the entrance foyer to the Centre des Expositions in Brussels is in the form of a hyperbolic paraboloid shell. Natural-colour aluminium, consisting of Kalzip 400 elements, on 100 mm glass wool thermal insulation constitutes the roof covering. The aluminium standing seam profiles, installed with «secret fixings» (clips which do not penetrate the roof), had their longitudinal folds made directly on site using a special machine. The fixing clips are provided with insulated caps to prevent thermal bridges; the clips easily accommodate the ensuing wind pressure and suction forces and allow the tray-shaped profiles to expand unhindered in the longitudinal direction. The non-riveted fixing clips type L-100 with their insulated caps, which attach the aluminium panels of the roof covering, are fixed to the galvanized steel trapezoidal profile roof decking onto which the vapour barrier is laid. The fixing clips penetrate the glass wool thermal insulation. The fixing points – above all at places subjected to heavy loads – are realized with the help of Omega profiles of galvanized steel (50 mm high) and by fixing the standing seam aluminium profiles to the clips with the aid of rivets. The shells of galvanized steel are connected to the primary structure of laminated timber, itself supported by reinforced concrete and timber columns. The whole construction covers an area of 26 000 m² on a grid measuring 15.0 x 16.2 m. Fascias, ridge, drainage and profile closures are made from folded aluminium.

Address: chaussée Romaine, Brussels, Belgium
Architects: Samyn & Partners, Brussels
Gh. André, Y. Avoiron, F. Berleur, B. de Man, J.-P. Dequenne, A. d'Udekem d'Acoz, F. el Sayed, T. Henrard, L. Kaisin, D. Mélotte, N. Milo, J.Y. Naimi, N. Neuckermans, T. Provoost, J.P. Rodriguez Samper, Q. Steyaert, P. Samyn, B. Thimister, G. van Breedam, M. Vandeput, S. Verhulst (project team architecture)
Consulting engineers: Samyn & Partners and Setesco – G. Clantin, L. Kaisin, J. Schiffmann, P. Samyn (structure);   Atenco, C. De Baeker (interior)
Client: Parc des Expositions de Bruxelles
Construction period: 1995-99
Aluminium components: Kalzip type 400 (65 x 400)
Fabricator: Hoogovens Aluminium International

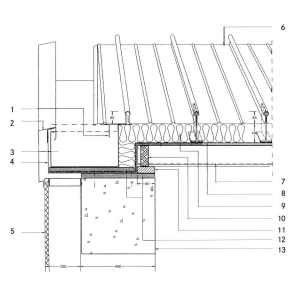

Eaves detail.
1   Gutter
2   Aluminium fascia
3   External aluminium gutter
4   Halpaco, folded
5   Metal on supporting frame
6   Kalzip profile
7   Galvanized steel decking
8   Vapour barrier
9   Thermal insulation
10 Filler piece
11 Timber wallplate
12 18 mm Multiplex
13 Beam

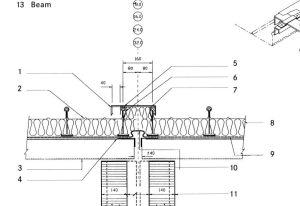

Expansion joint – axonometric view and section.
1   Profiled strip for concealing expansion joint
2   Kalzip profile
3   Galvanized structural sheeting
4   Internal strip, galvanized,
    joint opening max. 80 mm
5   Edge profile, clip fixing
6   Edge clip
7   5 mm aluminium plate, 900 mm spacing
8   Thermal insulation
9   Vapour barrier
10 Vapour barrier allowing for thermal expansion
11 Roof truss of laminated timber

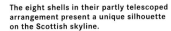
The eight shells in their partly telescoped
arrangement present a unique silhouette
on the Scottish skyline.

CONFERENCE CENTRE AND INDUSTRIAL THEATRE

Foster & Partners

Design: The continuing demand for space for organizing
international events is always associated with the increasing need
for space for presentations of all kinds. However, there are only a
few installations so flexible that they simultaneously offer facilities
for conferences, exhibitions, live shows, concerts and their
associated functions at all levels – from small-scale to global. The
Scottish Exhibition & Conference Centre in Glasgow is 40 m high,
140 m long and has 13 000 m² of usable floor area. It is the largest
such complex in the UK and one of only four in the whole of Europe
capable of accommodating more than 3000 congress attendees.
This impressive building with its roof of aluminium shells is located
in the industrial district of Clyde on the site of the former Queen's
Dock shipyard. The eight shells in their partly telescoped
arrangement present a unique silhouette on the Scottish skyline.
One of the most important constituents of the underlying concept
for this «industrial theatre» was the procurement of a neutral
setting (but with a full range of services) which would enable
organizers to use this facility for a huge variety of functions. The
conference halls on three levels have fixed seating for 3000
participants. The building has a fly tower and all other necessary
«backstage» facilities as well as the possibility of allowing large
goods vehicles to drive directly onto the stage. The main hall is not
only directly linked to the large exhibition areas, but also equipped
with an electronic voting system for congresses, a simultaneous
interpretation installation and audio-visual management facilities.
Visitors arrive on the east side of the centre. A broad glass facade
marks the entrance lobby. From here the visitor either moves
on directly to a smaller, 300-seat conference hall, or by way of

The glazed entrance facade at night.

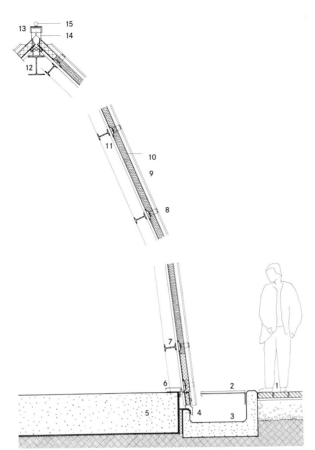

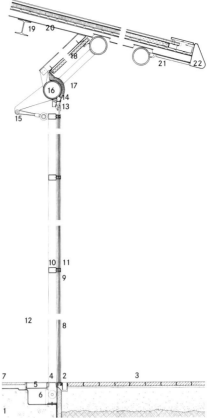

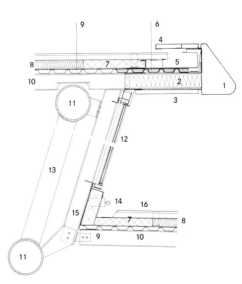

Section through roof construction.
1 200 x 100 x 60 mm mid-grey paving block on
   50 mm sand blinding
2 Open-grid galvanized steel drainage cover plate
3 Reinforced concrete (grade C50) drainage channel
4 1.2 mm stucco embossed aluminium base flashing
5 300 mm reinforced concrete ground floor slab
   on methane- and water-resistant membrane
6 Galvanized steel base fixing channel
7 152 x 89 mm galvanized steel secondary purlin
8 ST60 clips fixed to 1.6 mm galvanized steel top hat
9 305 mm wide Kalzip stucco embossed aluminium
   standing seam cladding
10 «Rockwool» 100 mm insulation quilt compressed to 80 mm
11 32 mm non-structural decking with «monarflex» vapour
   barrier laid over
12 254 x 254 mm steel top chord of triangular truss member,
   painted (colour: BS 00-A-09)
13 80 x 80 mm galvanized RHS ridge post with stucco
   embossed aluminium cover plate
14 Stucco embossed aluminium ridge flashing
15 Stainless steel eyebolt for latchway system fixed back
   to ridge post

**Section through entrance, junction between glass facade
and roof construction.**
1 100 mm rigid insulation sandwiched
   between gas membrane and DPM
2 Galvanized grille cover to perimeter drainage channel
3 200 x 100 x 60 mm mid-grey paving block on 50 mm
   sand blinding
4 152 x 89 mm galvanized RSC fixing plate
5 Aluminium perimeter heating grille
6 Perimeter heating element
7 600 x 600 mm «Charcon» internal paving slab
8 24 mm double glazed unit (6 mm toughened
   with low-E coating to third face, 12 mm cavity)
9 62.5 x 3 mm natural anodized aluminium pressure plate
10 150 x 100 mm RHS structural steel mullion, painted
   (colour: BS 00-A-09)
11 Transom channel comprising snap-in natural
   silver anodized aluminium sections
12 Structural steel bow-back mullion
13 25 mm natural silver anodized (both sides)
   aluminium sandwich panels
14 3 mm natural silver anodized aluminium cover strip
15 Cast stainless steel pin-jointed movement connection fixed
   to bottom boom of arch via 6 mm steel bracket
16 356 x 17.5 mm arch internal boom, painted
   (colour: BS 00-A-09)
17 3 mm PPC aluminium arch cover on 100 mm «Rockwool»
   insulation quilt compressed to 60 mm
18 75 mm «AME» plastisol-coated composite panel
19 254 x 254 mm steel primary purlin, painted
   (colour: BS 00-A-09)
20 152 x 89 mm galvanized steel secondary purlin
   (notched around arches)
21 0.9 mm aluminium PVF2A (metallic silver) soffit panels
22 Faceted 3 mm PPC aluminium bullnose

Detail of edge of shell and junction with shell below.
1 Faceted 3 mm PPC aluminium bullnose
2 «Rockwool» semi-rigid insulation
3 0.9 mm aluminium PVF2A (metallic silver) soffit panels
4 Faceted 2 mm PPC aluminium cover tray
5 Faceted gutter lined with «Sarnafil» waterproof membrane
6 «Rockwool» rigid profile fillers
7 «Rockwool» hard rock rigid insulation board
8 «Rockwool» 100 mm insulation quilt compressed to 80 mm
9 32 mm non-structural decking with «monarflex»
   vapour barrier laid over
10 152 x 89 mm galvanized steel secondary purlin
11 356 x 17.5 mm arch boom, painted
   (colour: BS 00-A-09)
12 75 mm double glazed module
13 193 x 8 mm arch internal bracing
14 Stucco embossed aluminium covering to latchway
   support system
15 152 x 89 mm galvanized steel arch cladding post
16 305 mm wide Kalzip 1.2 mm stucco embossed
   aluminium standing seam cladding

The shells are covered with an aluminium skin and are supported by galvanized steel purlins and trusses. The bullnose and the profiles above and below form the verges of the shells. The window frames in the glass facade are also made from natural silver anodized aluminium.

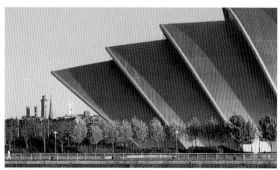

Side view of the roofs to the
Scottish Exhibition & Conference Centre
in Glasgow.

escalators and lifts to the first floor foyer. This foyer connects the three-storey main hall with the various exhibition facilities and leisure zones.

Construction: The powerful lines of the building, the materials used and the architectural details reflect the flexibility of utilization and the desire to minimize the cost of the building. The eight shells represent an economic enclosure for the main hall and its annexes. Indeed, the price per square metre (£ 1992) is really very low in comparison to traditional conference centres. The ten pointed arches comprising shallow trusses of circular hollow sections support the secondary purlins (I-sections of galvanized steel).

Materials: The entire area of 10 600 m² of the conference centre roof is covered with Kalzip aluminium panels installed with the help of «secret fixings» (clips which do not penetrate the construction). The longitudinal folds of these standing seam profiles were bent by machine directly on site. The insulated caps of the fixing clips prevent the formation of thermal bridges and the clips can reliably accommodate the wind pressure and suction forces which ensue, while at the same time allowing the unhindered longitudinal expansion of the tray-type panels. The clips penetrate the 100 mm layer of mineral wool which is thereby compressed to 80 mm. The thermal insulation and the clips are supported by galvanized steel trapezoidal profile sheeting (height 32 mm, thickness 0.7 mm). This layer is protected by a «monarflex» vapour barrier. The panels (thickness 1.2 mm, radius of curvature 38 m) were fabricated from Kal-Alloy (also known as Alclad). This material

Close-up of junction between glass facade and roof.

originally used in the aerospace industry consists of an aluminium alloy core (3004-AlMnMg 1) with an aluminium-zinc alloy (4 %) (AA7072-AlZn 1) protective plating to both faces. The granite stucco embossing to the aluminium alloy leads to a notable improvement in the durability of the exterior. The fixing points for the Kalzip elements, which are necessary to accommodate snow loads, are located on the apex of each pointed arch so that elongation due to thermal expansion takes place in the direction of the ground. Each shell level is made up of one half-arch consisting of a maximum of four consecutive sheets, which means that up to 14 m can be covered per side. The sheets were butt-welded on site (total length of weld seams 3.6 km). Rectangular aluminium sections (upper part 2 mm thick, lower part 0.9 mm) form the verges of the shells. An aluminium bullnose (3 mm thick) conceals a PVC drainage system which conveys rainwater diagonally to ground level where it is transported away in concrete culverts covered by a galvanized steel grid. The window frames in the glass facade are made from natural silver anodized aluminium.

Address: Scottish Exhibition and Conference Centre, Glasgow, Great Britain
Architects: Foster & Partners, London
Client: SECC Glasgow
Consulting engineers: Ove Arup (mechanical & electrical services, civil & structural engineering); Turner Townesend Project Management (project management)
Construction period: 1995-98
Aluminium components: Kalzip, Kal-Alloy type 305 (65 x 305)
Fabricator: Hoogovens Aluminium International

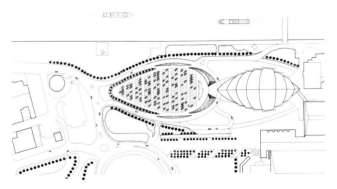
Site plan.

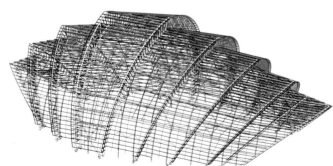
The principle of the roof construction.

Longitudinal section through the building.

The aluminium roof of the extension, which resembles a bird in flight, determines the shape of the structural elements. In contrast to this, the shape of the roof to the atrium is dominated by the frame from which the roof and the floors of this part of the building are suspended.

West facade.

Bracing to aluminium roof. Interplay of horizontal bands of aluminium panels and glazing with coloured glass.

Location map.

HONG KONG CONVENTION & EXHIBITION CENTER

SOM and Wong & Ouyang

Design: The new Hong Kong Convention & Exhibition Center (HKCEC) was built on an artificial island in Victoria Harbour. This is an extension to the existing centre; together, both buildings have a usable floor space of 150 000 m². The new building includes a 4500-seat congress hall, three exhibition halls with a total area of 28 000 m², two theatres, 52 meeting rooms, seven restaurants and other areas containing the necessary service facilities. An atrium measuring 120 m in length connects the new centre with the original building and offers supplementary exhibition space. The glazed circulation zones on the various levels offer magnificent views over the harbour and allow ample daylight to enter to illuminate these public spaces. The new extension was the site for the ceremonies of Great Britain's formal transfer of sovereignty to China in 1997.

The roof to the uppermost hall has a clear span of 80 m and is 14 m above the floor. Each of the three levels in the centre includes access for deliveries and supplies. Although the building was built on land reclaimed from the sea, the infrastructure requirements, e.g. tram network, planned underground line, had to be taken into account when planning the structure. The various curved roof surfaces of the HKCEC make it a monumental and sculptural element on Hong Kong's skyline. The wing-like 300 m long roof to the centre with its horizontal orientation forms a stark contrast to the prismatic verticality of the skyscrapers on the shore behind. Furthermore, it expresses the wish for stability integral to the Chinese spirituality. Feng Shui advisers were consulted several times during the planning phase for this project in order to guarantee that the cultural standards were being adhered to.

Main entrance.

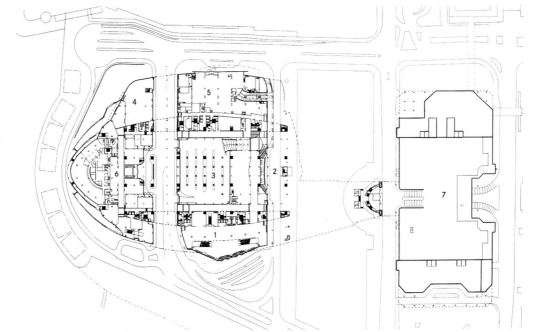

Plan of ground floor.
1   Main lobby
2   Bus drop-off
3   Truck marshalling
4   Restaurant
5   Administration
6   Retail
7   Existing building, loading docks

Framework supporting glass curtain wall, ceiling of aluminium panels.

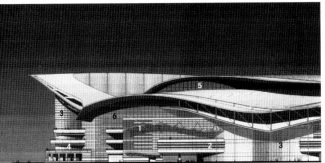

West facade
1 Vertical truss wall with tinted glass and aluminium panels
2 Glass, granite, and aluminium fins
3 Horizontal truss wall with clear glass
4 Glass fin wall
5 Louvre wall
6 Vertical truss wall with clear and tinted glass

Construction: As reinforced concrete structures can be built relatively inexpensively in Hong Kong, structural steel and concrete elements were combined in this project. This accelerated the construction. While the loadbearing walls of reinforced concrete were being cast on site, the roof trusses with their span of 80 m were being assembled in the Philippines with steel components fabricated in the UK or the USA. The roof trusses were brought to Hong Kong on barges and unloaded at a naval dock in the immediate vicinity of the site; they were then pulled to the site on rollers. These trusses support the main roof which covers the middle of the building and cantilevers out over the floors below.

The main architectural feature of the HKCEC is its roof construction, which reminds the observer of the outstretched wings of a bird. The geometry of this construction results from a «collage» of the various wings rotated, cut and joined together. From the highest roof level, supported by trusses every 14 m (13 principal trusses permit a clear span of 80 m), the various levels form a cascade down to the lowest canopies spanning over the main entrance for those arriving on foot in the west and over the entrance to the management offices in the east. All the roof trusses are unique owing to the shape of the roof. Secondary trusses spanning between the main trusses carry the roof covering. A series of structural steel elements, straight and prismatic, form loadbearing structures for each of the curved sections of the roof. These «bridge» elements are therefore neither arched nor curved. The vertical envelope of the building consists of curtain wall facades of aluminium and glass supported by horizontal and vertical tubular frames which in turn are carried by large-diameter columns. The steel horizontal frames, spaced corresponding to the height of the bands of glazing, span more than 13 m between the columns and carry the horizontal wind loads. The vertical frames are suspended from the roof on intermediate steel members and the vertical movements are accommodated by sliding frame members at the top of the first pane of glass. All frames are fixed at one end and have a sliding bearing at the other. This allows vertical movements to be accommodated; for the curtain walls must not only permit changes in length as a result of thermal effects due to solar radiation, they must also be able to accommodate the movements of the roof caused by severe wind loads (above all during typhoons).

Materials: Although maximum openness towards the surrounding environment is desirable here, it is necessary to reduce the amount of solar radiation entering the building in some areas by way of the roof cantilevers, the special layout of glazed areas and the aluminium sunshades. As a response to the diverse and varying conditions, the envelope of this extension to the HKCEC includes a number of different types of curtain wall, with clear glass in some areas and in other areas glazing with different degrees of opacity. Areas in which large numbers of people congregate were given maximum transparency so that visitors could enjoy the view over the harbour. Less transparency was necessary for those areas, e.g. the atrium, where visitors are primarily making their way from A to B in a horizontal or vertical direction. In places where maximum visibility is desirable, e.g. in the great 40 m high foyer or the main entrance which extends over several levels, bands of clear glass were included, supported by a delicate framework of tubular

Curtain wall and aluminium roofs.

View of Hong Kong Convention & Exhibition
Centre at night.

sections which do not obstruct the view of the surroundings.
The bands of glazing are interrupted by horizontal aluminium panels which function as sunshades. Areas of insulated aluminium panels alternate with green or blue glazing in those places subject to large amounts of solar radiation. The glazing elements butt-jointed on their vertical sides are fixed to horizontal frames at the end of each segment and in turn attached to vertical frames suspended from the roof construction.

The roof – from the innermost shell to the covering – consists of the metal «bridge» element described above (attached directly to the trusses), straight members and tension rods, thermal insulation, an arched metal grid connected directly to the flat fixing surfaces of the «bridge» element via height-adjustable fixings, concrete slabs, a single layer of vinyl foil, and a covering of braced aluminium. The areas of least curvature have flat aluminium panels fixed to the bracing. The extruded aluminium bracings (with internal water collector) are connected directly to the structural «bridge» element via the metal grid.

This type of construction is particularly advantageous with respect to the extreme loads caused by typhoons. During a typhoon, the quantity of precipitation per square metre is enormous; therefore, the drainage system has to be designed for such amounts of water. In this case the drainage system is located at the transitions between the various forms and at the edges of the roofs in order to carry the water away as quickly as possible. With such large surface areas, changes in length caused by thermal effects tend to be measured more in terms of centimetres than millimetres. Movements which take place transverse to the bracing can be accommodated by allowing the panels to flex slightly between the fixed bracing. However, movements in the longitudinal direction of the panels is harder to deal with because the individual panels are firmly jointed and the joints sealed to prevent ingress of water, above all in the flatter areas of the roof covering.

This problem was resolved by fixing the bracing in the middle to the supporting construction. This means that unhindered longitudinal movement in both directions is possible starting from this point. Expansion and contraction of the panels in the longitudinal direction was therefore confined to the areas of the rainwater gutters where the panels are supported without fixings. The disagreeable visual impact of the flexing of the aluminium panels was minimized by providing the panels with a V-shaped groove across their width. The two flanks of the V can close up as the panels expand or spread apart as the panels contract. Those panels with the smallest bending radius were given Z-fixings in the middle which also minimize the flexing.

PVDF-coated aluminium panels were chosen for reasons of cost and colour as well as durability. The noise of the rain striking the roof is attenuated by the addition of a sound-absorbent material attached to the inner surface of the aluminium panels and by covering the entire roof surface with a vinyl membrane. Concrete slabs form the underlay for the membrane and contribute through their mass to attenuating aircraft noise. In places where the underside of the roof construction is exposed, e.g. in the exhibition areas, aircraft noise is reduced by a combination of perforated plates and sound insulation.

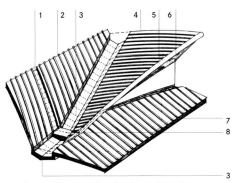

Perspective view of roof «bridge» element,
intersection of upper, mid and low roof levels.
1   600 mm wide reveal at grid lines
2   Upper roof
3   Stainless steel gutter
4   Mid roof
5   Silver aluminium «bullnose»
    at edges of roof wings
6   Silver aluminium soffit
7   Low roof
8   Waterstop

Address: Hong Kong, China
Architects: Wong & Ouyang;   Wo Hei Lam (director in charge);   Patrick S.K. Chung
(project architect); Si Hung Ha (deputy project architect);   Winston Sung, V.Y. Choong, Bing
Tung Lam (architectural design team); Ricardo Asis, May Wong (interiors);   Danny Tang, Ken
Montgomery, Mark Kelly, Jocelyn Chung, Sabrina Law, Raymond Fan, Stephen Valentine, Ralph
Walker, Pak Shun Lee, George Tang (project team)
Skidmore, Owings & Merrill (SOM);   Larry Oltmann (design partner);   Alan Hinklin
(project director); Paul DeVylder (project manager);   Ricard Smits (senior technical
coordinator);   Marshall Strabala (senior designer);   Dan Bell, Joe Castner, Sophie Dahdah,
Peter Freiberg, J.T. Hsu, Kamalrukh Katrak, Elizabeth Michalska, Ronald Ng, Dan Ringelstein
(project team)
Client: Hong Kong Trade Development Council
Consulting engineers: Skidmore, Owings & Merill;   Stan Korista, Ron Johnson,
Srinivasa Iyengar, Robert Halvorson, Tim Kaye, David McLean, Raul Pacheco (structure);
Heitmann & Associates (external wall and roof cladding);   SL & A Graphics (graphics and
signage);   PHA Lighting Design, Fisher Marantz Renfro Stone (lighting);   James Carpenter
(sculpture in main lobby)
Construction period: 1991-97
Aluminium components: PVDF-coated aluminium (roof)
Fabricators: Builder's Federal, United Reliance (curtain wall of metal, glass and stone);
Builder's Federal, Weatherwise (aluminium roof covering)

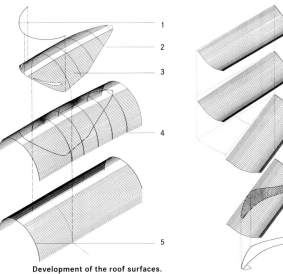

Development of the roof surfaces.
1   «Cookie cutter»: cut edge of vault using clipping
    geometry or «cookie cutter»
2   Mid roof intersection: intersect vault with mid roof
    and low roof geometries
3   Low roof intersection
4   «Break» vault at grid lines, tilt each vault segment down
5   Profile designed by series of tangent arcs, extrude profile
    to create vault

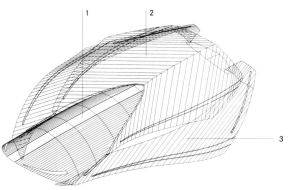

Computer model for upper roof level.
1   Upper roof
2   Mid roof
3   Low roof

Vertical and horizontal sections through
curtain wall structure.
1   Clear glass handrail
    with stainless steel cap
2   Cruciform steel struts
3   Steel tie rods
4   Double steel front plates
5   Double steel back plates
6   Aluminium mullion
7   Tinted (green) glass
8   Embossed aluminium panel
9   Rigid steel tubular bracing
10 Rigid steel tubular bracing
11 Steel tubular tie
12 Glass panel
13 Steel or concrete structural column

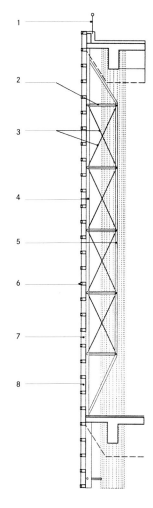

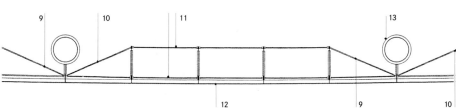

The «whale» on the roof of the building.

ING BANK & NNH HEADOFFICES

(EEA) Erick van Egeraat associated architects

Design: This building in Andrássy Street is one of a number of city-centre buildings with an inner courtyard which, despite the many changes which Budapest has undergone over the course of history, has remained intact. Built in 1882, this building shows evidence of the influences of the neo-Renaissance period. It has been scrupulously restored and enhanced by contemporary elements, one of which is the glass roof spanning over the inner courtyard. The building, complemented and upgraded by the addition of these new elements, can be regarded as an optimistic symbol for the current upheavals in Central Europe. The concept developed here is far removed from any form of hackneyed historicism and, furthermore, is receptive to innovation and revitalization. At the same time, we can regard it as one of the first buildings in which the juxtaposition of uncompromising modernism and intuitive organic forms gives rise to an architecture which could be called «modern Baroque». The presence of the «whale» gives the conference hall an organic form which can be felt everywhere in this old building even though the «whale» is never seen in its entirety. Like an air bubble it floats on the «sea» of glass. The inner courtyard is flooded with light and is given an indescribable presence/absence which fascinates and intrigues the visitor. The building forces a paroxysm of dialogue between old and new, order and freedom, linearity and curvature, earth and sky, the classical techniques of monumental construction and the technologies of web-like skins.

Construction and materials: The new interventions essentially consist of a framework of I-sections, beams of rolled glass, arches

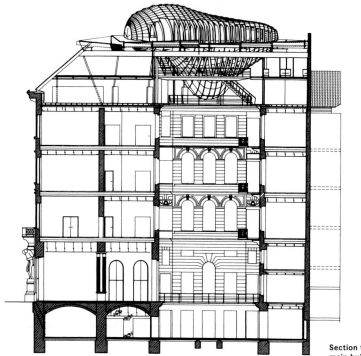

Section through refurbished
main building.

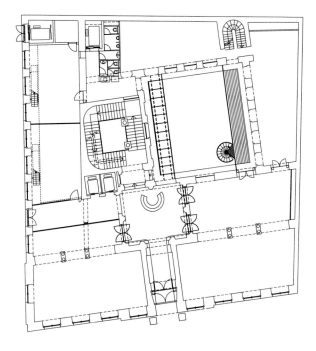

Plan of ground floor.

Plan of roof.

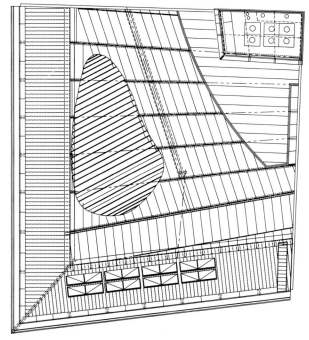

The refurbished building dating from 1882.

Night-time view of the «sea» of glass over the conference hall.

Interior view of inner courtyard showing
the «belly» of the «whale».

The aluminium frames for the glazing of
the «whale».

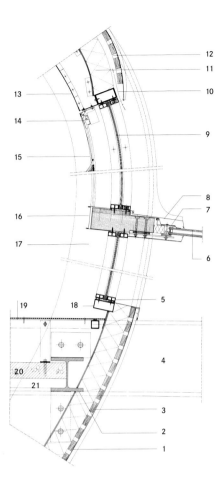

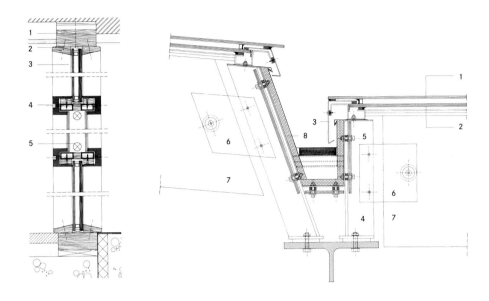

Detail of aluminium sign mountings.
1 Teak frame
2 Teak glazing bead
3 Insulating glazing
4 Fixing for aluminium sign
5 Neon lighting

Detail of glass roof at eaves.
1 Wired glass
2 Wired glass, multilayer
3 Anodized aluminium section
4 Stainless steel support
5 Profiled glass element
6 Stainless steel connection
7 Rolled glass beam
8 Insulated steel panel

The covering to the «whale».
1 Zinc supporting grid
2 HE 160B
3 Zinc covering
4 NE 360A beam
5 Aluminium glazing beads,
   20 x 40 x 3 mm
6 Glazing
7 EPDM foil
8 Zinc hood
9 Curved glass
10 Ventilation under zinc element
11 100 mm mineral wool
12 Ventilation duct
13 Inner cladding
14 Motorized sunshade
15 Sunshade
16 Zinc
17 Laminated timber arch
   (6 mm laminations)
18 Aluminium hollow section,
   50 x 100 x 5 mm
19 Perforated 4 mm steel sheet
20 Reinforced concrete floor
21 Steel profile sheeting

of laminated timber (the «whale»), a roof covering of glass and zinc elements as well as stainless steel components. Aluminium is simply reserved for certain frame elements for the glazing and for certain assemblies, e.g. the fixed frame for the «whale», which consists of curved aluminium rectangular hollow sections (50 x 100 x 5 mm) with glazing beads also made from aluminium rectangular hollow sections (20 x 40 x 3 mm). The sign mountings above the doors facing the street are also made from aluminium.

Address: Andrássy út, Budapest, Hungary
Architects: (EEA) Erick van Egeraat associated architects
Savany & Partners, Budapest (associated architects);   Erick van Egeraat, Tibor Gall (architects);
Maartje Lammers (project architect);   Gábor Kruppa (project leader);   Astrid Huwald, János
Tiba, Stephen Moylan, William Richards, Ineke Dubbeldam, Miranda Nieboer, Harry Boxelaar,
Tamara Klassen, Atilla Komjathy, Dianne Anyka (project team)
Interior design: (EEA) Erick van Egeraat associated architects
Client: Nationale Nederlanden Vastgoed, The Hague;   Nationale Nederlanden Hungary
Ltd, Budapest;   ING Bank, Budapest
Consulting engineers: Pro plan Kft;   Munk Dunstones Associates, London (quantity surveyors);
ABT Adviesburo voor Bouwtechniek b.v., Delft (structure);   Ketel Raadgevende Ingenieurs b.v.,
Delft (installations)
Construction period: 1992-94
Fabricator: Permasteelisa Italia; Hydro Alluminio Ornago, Milan (aluminium production)

The Paulay-Ede Street facade reflects the buildings opposite.

View of the extension at night. On the right the facade with the «natural stone» elements evokes the rhythm of the original building dating from 1882.

EXTENSION TO
ING BANK & NNH HEADOFFICES

(EEA) Erick van Egeraat associated architects

Design: The new office building is an extension to the modernized neo-Renaissance building in Andrássy Street. On one side the extension is a direct continuation of the rendered and decorated facade of the old building and so the rhythm of the fenestration of the bays of the old building are repeated and continued in the new facade according to the stipulations of the historic monuments authority. The dimensions of the new block as well as its position made the choice of a glazed curtain wall virtually automatic so that daylight levels in the interior would comply with the building code. Individual offices are located along Paulay-Ede Street on the various floors. Pivoting glass partitions parallel to the street can be used to separate these offices from the open-plan zones. The stairs suspended on stainless steel cables constitute the sole «highlight» of the interior architecture.

Construction and materials: Rather than just reproduce the old facade, a new technique is applied to the glazed curtain wall (structural glazing): every second element is printed with a computer pixels motif by means of silk screen printing so that from a certain distance it resembles a natural stone surface. As we approach the building, this impression is transformed and we perceive the translucent stippling of the glass screen. This technique permits daylight to penetrate deep into the interior. The Paulay-Ede Street elevation is fully glazed and so reflects the simple facades of the buildings opposite. It is a twin-leaf, climate-control construction. Exhaust-air from inside passes through the cavity between the inner and outer leaves, thus improving the thermal properties of the envelope. The inside face of the double glazing of

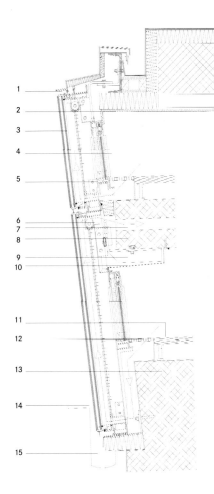

Detail of twin-leaf facade.
1 Aluminium flashing
2 Climate-control ceiling
3 Double glazing with «natural stone» appearance
4 Sliding door
5 Aluminium structure
6 Motorized sunshades
7 Ventilation duct
8 Reinforced concrete floor
9 Galvanized section
10 Aluminium cover
11 Raised floor
12 Stainless steel grille
13 Reinforced concrete floor over basement
14 Street level
15 Channel for water draining from the street

Section through refurbished main building and new extension.

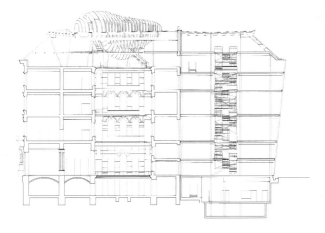

Every second facade element is silk screen printed so that from a certain distance it resembles a natural stone surface.

the outer leaf is provided with a pattern using silk screen printing to provide privacy for the occupants. The floors of the building comprise a large grid with a percentage of perforations for the air-conditioning system incorporated above the ceiling panels.

Address: Paulay Ede utca, Budapest, Hungary
Architects: (EEA) Erick van Egeraat associated architects;   Erick van Egeraat (architect);   Maartje Lammers (project architect);   Gábor Kruppa, János Tiba, Axel Koshany, Paul-Martin Lied, William Richards, Dianne Anyka, Emmet Scanlon, Zoltan Király (project team)
Interior design: (EEA) Erick van Egeraat associated architects
Client: ING Real Estate International, The Hague
Consulting engineers: ADAM-management-consultants, Budapest; MDA Overseas Ltd, Croydon (quantity surveyors);   ABT Adviesburo voor Bouwtechniek b.v., Delft and Mérték Epitészeti Studio, Budapest (structure);   Ove Arup & Partners, London (installations)
Construction period: 1992-97
Aluminium components: aluminium used for the curtain wall: alloy AA 6060 T5; anodizing process for the sections: cold-anodizing, coating depth 20 μm, natural silver colour
Fabricator: Permasteelisa Italia;   Hydro Alluminio Ornago, Milan (aluminium production)

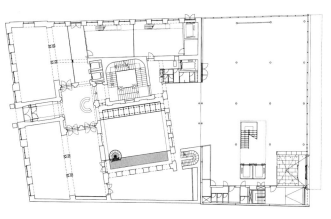

Plan of ground floor – old building and extension.

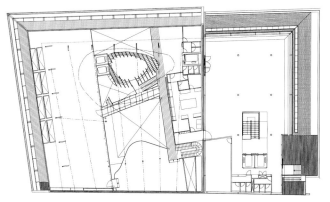

Plan view of mezzanine floor below the roofs of the old and new buildings.

The inclined, twin-leaf, climate-control facade on Paulay-Ede Street.

Interior view. The rhythm of the glass elements prolongs the rhythm of the original building.

View of the IHR complex.

The south facade facing the port.

ICHTHUS COLLEGE

(EEA) Erick van Egeraat associated architects

Design: The new building for the Ichthus Hogeschool Rotterdam (IHR), situated directly adjacent to the Erasmus Bridge on the Kop van Zuid peninsula in Rotterdam, makes references to the specific industrial character of the port architecture of the late 19th and early 20th centuries. The architecture tends to be dictated by the unique location and the orientation of the building rather than by the various functions it contains. On the scale of the city, the port constitutes the principal reference for the IHR; on a local scale, the building fits in with its immediate environment. For instance, the arcades of the neighbouring building are continued on the ground floor. The first three floors contain rooms provided for special uses. The standard classrooms on the six floors above are for conventional, traditional methods of teaching. These floors are highly flexible because they may be divided up by partitions. Above the terraced floor of the first storey there is an atrium which extends the full height of the building behind the south facade. This atrium is the very heart of the building and contains study areas for students. From here there is a unique view of the port. This central open space permeates the IHR building and so all those working there sense a bond with the heart of the building. On the garden side there is a terrace whose calm, contemplative nature represents a contrast to the hustle and bustle of the port.

Construction: The building measures 76.65 x 34.60 m on plan. The column spacing along the length of the building is regular, but across it the column spacing varies to suit the layout. The floors are prefabricated reinforced concrete planks. Steel is the material used for the majority of columns and beams as well as the roofing

The internal atrium with internal curtain wall facade; certain modules have a cobalt blue printing.

(trapezoidal profile sheeting). Some floors are supported conventionally, others are suspended from a steel tension rod construction.

Materials: The prevailing material of the IHR is glass: clear glass and glass with a cobalt blue printing. The use of glass echoes the architecture of the port and lends the building a great transparency, optimum flexibility and, at the same time, permits a remarkable view of the surroundings. The extruded aluminium sections manufactured in Korea were given a special anodized surface treatment: they were first given a matt finish before being immersed in the anodizing bath for two hours. There are two types of extruded aluminium frames: with drained joints on the curtain wall of the garden facade and on the inside of the facades, and with decorated joints in the form of «aircraft half-wings» on the port facade to emphasize the horizontal orientation of this elevation. The cable ducts and suspension arrangement for the louvre blinds are integrated in the frames. The curtain wall on the side of the administration tower is a climate-control, twin-leaf facade. The air in the cavity is circulated and passes into the ducts in the ceilings. Louvre blinds are positioned in the cavity and openings to permit cleaning and maintenance of the cavity are incorporated in the inner leaf. The opening lights cannot be distinguished from the fixed (structural) glazing, which helps to maintain the flush, structured appearance of the facade. Timber elements are also used in the interior.

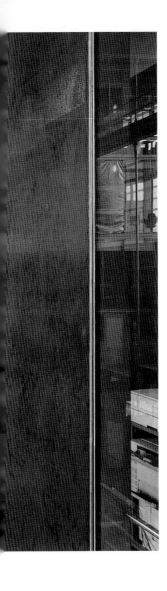

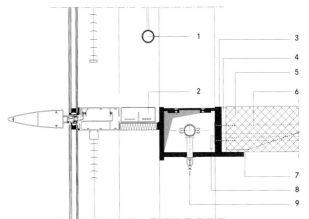

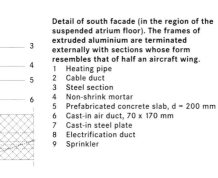

Detail of south facade (in the region of the suspended atrium floor). The frames of extruded aluminium are terminated externally with sections whose form resembles that of half an aircraft wing.

1 Heating pipe
2 Cable duct
3 Steel section
4 Non-shrink mortar
5 Prefabricated concrete slab, d = 200 mm
6 Cast-in air duct, 70 x 170 mm
7 Cast-in steel plate
8 Electrification duct
9 Sprinkler

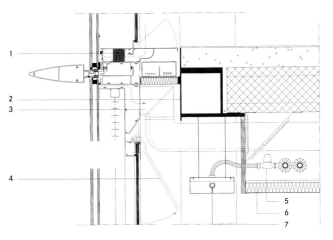

Detail of south facade in administration tower; curtain wall (climate-control, twin-leaf) facade.

1 Air filter
2 Steel section
3 Air duct
4 Climate-control facade
5 Thermostat
6 Perforated steel ceiling
7 Heating

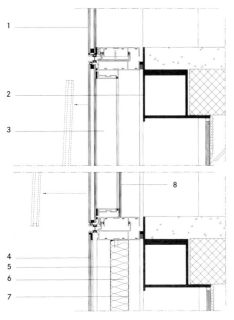

Detail of garden facade.

1 Structural glazing
2 Steel section
3 Structural glazing window
4 Structural glazing with silk screen printing
5 Fibreglass blanket
6 Insulation
7 Galvanized steel inner panel
8 Glass banister

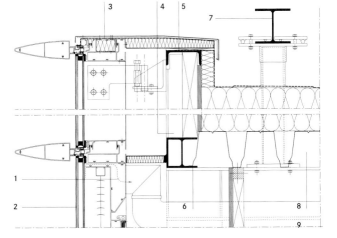

Junction between edge of roof and south facade.

1 Air extract of climate-control facade
2 Climate-control facade
3 Aluminium flashing
4 HE 140 A
5 UNP 160
6 HE 180 A
7 Facade cleaning system
8 Steel roof construction
9 HE 240 A

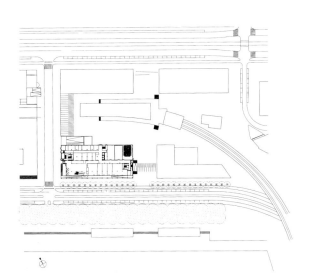

Site plan of IHR.

Detail of curtain wall with perforated aluminium panels underneath.
The thermal insulation (galvanized steel sheet inside/thermal
insulation/glass fibre covering outside) is attached behind the double
glazing of the facade.

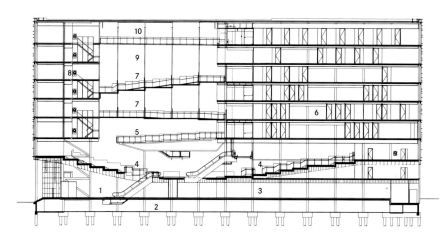

Longitudinal section.
1   Entrance lobby
2   Parking
3   Shops
4   Terraced restaurant
5   Study area
6   Offices and flexible work spaces
7   Suspended study area
8   Administration tower
9   Atrium
10 Suspended bridge

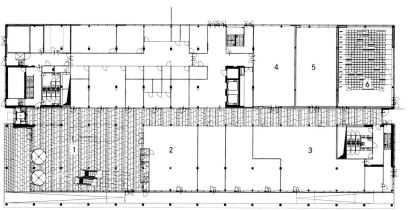

Plan of ground floor.
1   Entrance lobby
2   Bookshop
3   Copy shop
4   Workroom
5   Dance and drama
6   Lecture theatre
7   Lift

Interior view.

Address: Veemstraat, Rotterdam, Netherlands
Architects: (EEA) Erick van Egeraat associated architects;
Erick van Egeraat, Maartje Lammers, Monica Adams (architects); Maartje Lammers, Monica Adams (project architects); Maartje Lammers (project director); Kerstin Hahn, Colette Niemeijer, Lisette Magis, Ramon Knoester, Nienke Booy, Folkert van Hagen, Perry Klootwijk, Joep van Etten, Ard Buijsen, Pavel Fomenko, Harry Kurzhals, Paul-Martin Lied, Karolien de Pauw, Stefanie Schleich, Boris Zeisser (competition project team); Cock Peterse, Jeroen ter Haar, Luc Reyn, Paul Blonk, Mika Lundberg, Kerstin Hahn, Colette Niemeijer, Ronald Ubels, Jos Overmars, Ezra Buenrostro-Hoogwater, Matthias Frei, Claudia Radinger, Ole Schmidt, Rowan van Wely, Sabrina Kers, Sara Hampe, Julia Hausmann, Bas de Haan, Aude de Broissia (implementation project team)
Interior design: (EEA) Erick van Egeraat associated architects
Client: IHR Ichthus Hogeschool Rotterdam
Consulting engineers: Berenschot Osborne b.v., Utrecht; ABKS, Arnhem (quantity surveyors); ABT Adviesburo voor Bouwtechniek b. v., Delft/Arnhem (structure, mechanical and electrical services); Adviesbureau Peutz & Associes b.v., Mook (acoustics); European Fire Protection consultants, Bilthoven (fire protection)
Construction period: 1996-2000
Fabricator: Scheldebouw, Middelburg (facades)

View of the building showing
the entrance.

West facade.

Ground floor windows and external access stairs.

KIKUTAKE ARCHITECTS OFFICE

Kikutake Architects

Design: This five-storey building contains a garage, offices and two apartments. The project makes use of various options for saving energy and, as a prototype for the ecological office building of the future, also encompasses the conception of open rooms flooded with daylight. If it is to serve as the model building for the 21st century, in harmony with the natural environment, then it must comply with five basic principles:
– The use of daylight and natural ventilation.
– The use of a building envelope (glass building with twin-leaf facade) with passive energy features in order to exploit the ensuing heat.
– The use of glazed facades depending on the orientation (architecture with passive use of solar energy).
– The use of electricity generated by photovoltaic panels on the roof.
– The provision of hot water by means of solar energy.
Applying these principles when building new office blocks or refurbishing existing buildings enables them to be realized in line with ecological aspects, acting as examples for sustainable development and optimization of the use of environmentally compatible forms of energy.

Construction: The reinforced concrete construction is based on a dual grid measuring 8 x 6 m and 8 x 4 m (going from west to east). The glass construction extending over four storeys is on the south side and contributes to considerable heat gains in the offices and two apartments. Aluminium sunshades reflect the solar radiation on the west side. This mechanism and the low thermal transmission achieved by the high degree of efficiency of the thermal break in the double glazing as well as the low emissivity of the glazing itself ensure that excessive heating of the air inside the building is avoided. This is achieved with minimal energy usage. On the north side insulating double glazing with a high degree of efficiency and low emissivity guarantees the necessary thermal insulation and maintains the required level of comfort. Owing to the specific properties of the double glazing, it is possible to absorb the energy of the (short wave) solar radiation but conserve the (long wave) internal heat energy by way of refraction.

Address: Bunkyo-ku, Tokyo, Japan
Architects: Kikutake Architects
Client: Design Research Company
Consulting engineers: Takenaka Corpor (structure); Kandenko Company, Nishihara Engineering Company, Takasago Thermal Engineering Company (mechanical and electrical services)
Construction: 1997
Aluminium components: sunshades of aluminium type JIS (Japan Industrial Standard) 4000 Λ1100P, baked acrylic paint finish, permissible wind pressure: 2058 Pa
Fabricators: Sky Aluminium Company (aluminium); Asahi Kinzoku Kogyo Company (aluminium louvre sunshades)

Sunshades on the west facade and glass on the south.

Section through sunshades, 3 mm aluminium sheet.

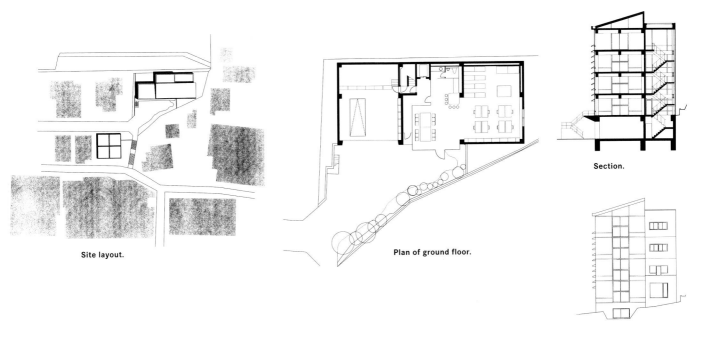

Site layout.

Plan of ground floor.

Section.

South elevation (with vertical glazing).

Index of Names and Places

Illustration Credits